FROM EZRA TO THE LAST

OF THE MACCABEES

FROM EZRA
TO THE LAST OF THE
MACCABEES

FOUNDATIONS OF POST-BIBLICAL JUDAISM

ELIAS BICKERMAN

SCHOCKEN BOOKS · NEW YORK

PUBLISHER'S NOTE

The present volume combines Professor Elias Bickerman's two major studies on the period: "The Historical Foundations of Postbiblical Judaism," originally published in 1949 in *The Jews: Their History, Culture, and Religion*, edited by Louis Finkelstein and reprinted with the permission of the editor and Harper & Brothers; and *The Maccabees: An Account of Their History from the Beginnings to the Fall of the House of the Hasmoneans*, originally published in 1947 by Schocken Books in its Library series. Chapter VII of the "Historical Foundations" has been omitted, since its contents duplicates in part the presentation in *The Maccabees*. With this exception the two studies complement each other.

PART II WAS TRANSLATED FROM THE GERMAN
BY MOSES HADAS

First SCHOCKEN PAPERBACK edition 1962
10 9 8   81 82 83 84

Manufactured in the United States of America
ISBN 0-8052-0036-3

CONTENTS

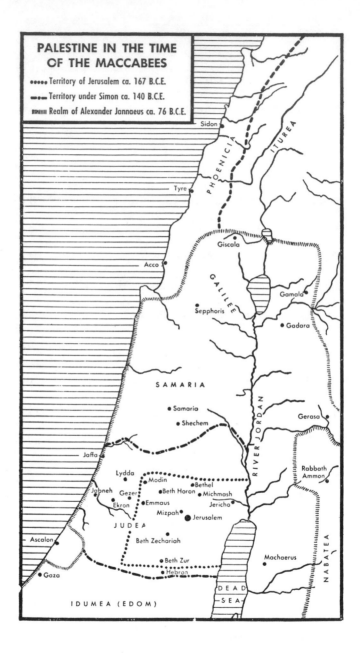

PALESTINE IN THE TIME OF THE MACCABEES

••••• Territory of Jerusalem ca. 167 B.C.E.
—•—• Territory under Simon ca. 140 B.C.E.
▥▥▥▥ Realm of Alexander Jannaeus ca. 76 B.C.E.

Sidon

PHOENICIA

ITUREA

Tyre

Giscala

GALILEE

Acco

Gamala

Sepphoris

Gadara

SAMARIA

Samaria

Gerasa

Shechem

RIVER JORDAN

Jaffa

Lydda

Rabbath
Ammon

Modin

Bethel

Jabneh

Gezer

Beth Horon

Michmash

Ekron

Emmaus

Jericho

Mizpah

Jerusalem

JUDEA

Ascalon

Beth Zechariah

NABATEA

Beth Zur

Machaerus

Gaza

Hebron

DEAD
SEA

IDUMEA (EDOM)

PART I

THE HISTORICAL FOUNDATIONS OF

POST-BIBLICAL JUDAISM

I

THE RETURN FROM

THE BABYLONIAN EXILE

The sacred history of the Chosen People ends
chronologically with Nehemiah's prayer: "Remember us, O God, for good." With Nehemiah's name,
"glorious in his memory," concludes the praise of
the worthies in the Wisdom of Ben Sira, composed
in Jerusalem about 190 B.C.E. Thus, even before the
Maccabean revolt, the Jews recognized that after
Nehemiah and his contemporary prophets, that is,
toward the end of the fifth century, in the age of
Socrates, the postbiblical period of Jewish history
begins. That period is marked by a unique and
rewarding polarity: on the one hand, the Jerusalem
center and, on the other, the plurality of centers
in the Diaspora. The Dispersion saved Judaism
from physical extirpation and spiritual inbreeding.
Palestine united the dispersed members of the nation and gave them a sense of oneness. This
counterpoise of historical forces is without analogy
in antiquity. There were, of course, numberless

migrations and transportations of peoples and fragments of peoples; but in due time these offshoots lost connection with the main stock. The colonists brought to cities of Syria by Assyrian kings, the men of Cutha or of Erech, were very soon detached psychologically from their respective cities. Likewise, Phoenician or Greek settlements soon separated from the metropolis. At the most, the Phoenicians had refused to follow a Persian king in his campaign against Carthage, their colony.[1] But the Jewish Dispersion continued to consider Jerusalem as the "metropolis" (Philo), turned to the Holy Land for guidance, and in turn, determined the destinies of its inhabitants. Men who established the normative Judaism in Palestine—Zerubbabel, Ezra, Nehemiah—came from the Diaspora, from Babylon and Susa.

The forces which unwittingly enabled Israel to develop into a people alike at home in the ancestral land as well as in the lands of the Dispersion were largely external. When Jerusalem was conquered (597 B.C.E.) and, later (586), destroyed by the Babylonians, the court, the warriors, the craftsmen were transferred to Mesopotamia. This device of deportation, invented perhaps by the Hittites, and applied subsequently by all their successors (Babylonians, Persians, Greeks, Romans, Turks and even Anglo-Americans—as readers of Longfellow's *Evangeline* know) was by no means an attempt at extermination. The distortion of the ancient expedient is an invention of a modern, European nation in the twentieth century. Being Semites and idolators, the Babylonians simply transported a rebellious group elsewhere in order to break its natural cohesion. In new surroundings, mixed with other ethnic elements, the former enemy learned obedience and, once subdued, furnished labor, taxes and military services. Accordingly, the exiles received land to till, abandoned sites to rebuild and to settle.[2] They remained free and mostly under leadership of native chiefs. Such a *segan* (as he is called in Aramaic documents) of Phrygians, of Carians, etc., is often mentioned in cuneiform records from Babylonia. On the other hand, since the structure of Oriental monarchies was essentially feudal, there was neither the wish nor the need to assimilate. Thus, in 331 B.C.E., there was still near Nippur (in Mesopotamia) a Carian settlement of colonists transported there from Asia Minor at least two hundred years before. Likewise, the Captivity had created numerous Jewish settlements in Mesopotamia. As a later Babylonian historian tells us (according to some lost original records), King Nebuchadnezzar assigned to the captives dwelling

5

places "in the most convenient districts of Babylonia."[8] Later, in 539, when the Persian king Cyrus conquered Babylon, he reversed, quite naturally, the policy of his adversary and allowed gods and men in Babylonian captivity to return home.

At this moment, the restoration of the Holy City, burned fifty years previously, depended on an accidental conjunction. When the Assyrians conquered Samaria in 722 they established a military colony there. As a result, the Ten Tribes, deported to Assyria, could never again come back. Since, however, there were already military colonies of the Assyrians in Palestine (Samaria, Gezer, etc.), Nebuchadnezzar did not need to send new settlers to Jerusalem. Further, although the Babylonians were savage in battle, they took no delight in useless destruction and wholesale slaughter. The remnant of Judah was not exterminated or scientifically tortured to death. Nobody desecrated the graves in Jerusalem; nobody prevented the believers from bringing meal offerings and frankincense to the burned-down House of the Lord and from weeping on its ruins. The walls of Jerusalem being broken down by the Babylonians, the ancient capital was now an open Jewish village. So, unlike the case of Samaria, there was a political vacuum

6

which the Restoration could fill. In the same manner, for example, the Thebans, dispersed by Alexander the Great (in 334), returned eighteen years later and rebuilt their commonwealth.[4] The exceptional feature of Jewish history is the reluctance of so many of the exiled to go back. They remained in Mesopotamia but, paradoxically, continued to care for the Holy City generation after generation, for centuries and millennia. Cupbearer before Artaxerxes I, born and reared in the fifth generation in the Diaspora, Nehemiah weeps when he hears of the affliction of the Children of Israel in Jerusalem. He risks disgrace to obtain royal favor for the Holy City. How are we to explain this unity between the Dispersion and Jerusalem?

Every transferred group continued, as a matter of course, to worship the ancestral gods on foreign soil. The men of Cutha, transplanted to Samaria, worshiped Nergal, and the men of Sepharvaim in Samaria continued to sacrifice their children to Adrammelech and Anamelech (II Kings 17:30).[5] "The Jewish force" in Elephantine, mercenaries established there by the Pharaohs about 600 B.C.E.,[6] continued to worship the national God on the southern frontier of Egypt. On the other hand, as a matter of course, the colonists feared and worshiped gods of the land in which they dwelt. A priest of Beth-el was sent back from the Captivity to teach the Assyrian colonists in the land of Samaria how to serve the God of Israel. But the latter was a "jealous God." Some Jews at Elephantine, the seat of the Egyptian god Khnum, seem to have accepted this sheep-headed divinity, or other pagan deities. But even to them the God of Zion, "Yahu" or "Yahu Sabaot," as they styled Him, remained the supreme divinity.[7]

The Diaspora clung to its unique God and to Jerusalem, the unique center of lawful worship. But at the same time, the God of Zion, the "great and terrible God," was not only the God of the Jews; He was the sole God in heaven and earth, the so-called deities of the pagans were nothing but vain idols. Hence, the polarity of Jerusalem and the Dispersion had its ideological counterpart in the paradoxical combination of universal monotheism and particularism, in the conception that the sole Lord of the Universe dwells on the hillock of Zion. This theological paradox held the Jews in the Dispersion together, and from all points of the compass they directed their eyes to the Lord's Temple in Jerusalem.

But here, in turn, we have to consider the political aspect of the situation. The spiritual unity of the Jews could hardly be established around Jerusalem if the whole Orient, from the Indus to Ethiopia, had not been one world obeying the orders issued by the Persian king. By its influence at the royal court, the Diaspora in Babylonia and Persia could act in behalf of Jewry everywhere and impose a uniform standard of faith and behavior. In a papyrus unearthed in Elephantine we can still read a communication, sent in 419, to the Jewish settlement at this other end of the world, giving rules as to the observance of the Feast of Unleavened Bread. These instructions were forwarded to the satrap of Egypt by King Darius of Persia. On the other hand, in their troubles with the Egyptians, the Jews in Elephantine wrote to the Jewish authorities in Jerusalem.

Or again, the re-establishment of normative Judaism after the Exile is connected by both Jewish tradition and modern scholarship with the name of Ezra, who restored the Law of Moses. But unlike Moses, Ezra's authority to promulgate and administer the Torah in Jerusalem was not derived from a Divine Revelation. Ezra arrived at Jerusalem as a Persian commissioner with a royal letter placing "the Law of thy God" on the same compulsory level as the law of the king, and threatening the offender of Mosaic precepts with death, banishment, confiscation of goods and imprisonment. In this way the perpetual character of the Torah was established and the Divine Law made known and imposed on all Jewry under the Persian scepter. When, after the dissolution of the empire of Alexander the Great, about 300 B.C.E., the unity of the political world of which the Jews were part had been broken, the religious and spiritual cohesion remained firmly established on the foundations laid down during the Persian age by Ezra and Nehemiah, King Darius and King Artaxerxes.

The imperial protection shielded Palestinian Jewry from the Arabs and the Philistines, Edom and Moab. In the background of Jewish history in Palestine, from the time of the Judges, there was a constant drive of Aramaic and Arab nomads against the settled country whose comforts they envied. Persian, and later, Macedonian, frontier guards secured from now on the peace of the Jewish peasant. If Jerusalem had not been a part of a Gentile empire, the nomads would have driven the Jews into the sea or swallowed up Palestine, and the rock of Zion would have been the foundation of an Arabian sanctuary a thousand years before Omar's mosque.

THE JUDAISM OF EZRA

AND THE CHRONICLER

———

Let us now take a look at Judaism in the last century of Persian rule, after Nehemiah (432) and before Alexander's conquest of Asia (332). During this period, Jerusalem and a strip of land around it formed a small district of Judea *(Yehûd)* lost in the enormous satrapy "Across the River," that is, west of the Euphrates. The district of Judea was approximately a quadrilateral, about thirty-five miles long, from Beth-el to Beth-zur, and from twenty-five to thirty miles broad, the plateau between the Dead Sea and the lowland in the west. Its area was about a thousand square miles, of which a good part was desert. Of the political history of Judea during our period there is virtually no record. An accidental notice informs us that Artaxerxes III of Persia had deported many Jews to the Caspian Sea during his campaign against Egypt. In all probability, Jerusalem, like Sidon, sided with Egypt in this conflict. A cuneiform tablet

11

records the transport of prisoners from Sidon to Babylonia in the autumn of 345.[8] Thirteen years later Jerusalem as well as Sidon opened the gates to Alexander the Macedonian.

There was a Persian governor in Jerusalem; there was a provincial fiscus; jar handles bearing stamps of "Judea" and "Jerusalem" in Hebrew (and later Aramaic) characters show that tribute was paid in kind.[9] The governors received "bread and wine" from the people (Neh. 5:15) and since the governor had to provide a free table for his officers and the nobles of the land, each day he had to slay one ox and six choice sheep, exclusive of fowl. No wonder, then, that the governor expected a sheep as a present in behalf of suppliants (Mal. 1:8). Monetary economy, nevertheless, began to grow in Palestine. In the time of Nehemiah there are people borrowing money to pay the royal taxes. It is worth noting that Persian royal coins have not been found until now in the numerous and rich coin hoards of the fourth century in this region.[10] Likewise, the Book Ezra-Nehemiah does not mention any coin; when it mentions precious metals and objects made of the metals, it reports their weight. There is no certain record of troops from Judea in Persian service. The contingent from "the Solymian hills" in Xerxes' expedition against

Greece, mentioned in the epic poem of Choerilus, a friend of Herodotus, refers probably to the "eastern Ethiopians." But the Jews had arms and had to appear with their swords, their spears and their bows by order of the governor. The latter had his personal guard, and the castle in which he lived commanded the Temple Hill.

Like every city and nation in the Persian Empire the Jews enjoyed a more or less large autonomy, amplified by bribes and diminished from time to time by arbitrary interference of the Persian authorities. For instance, when once a murder had been committed in the Temple, the governor inflicted on the Jewish nation the fine of fifty shekels for every lamb used in the daily offering; this payment was enforced for seven years, that is, probably, until a new governor came to Jerusalem. The Jews were represented by "the nobles of the Jews," the heads of the clans. On the other hand, there was the High Priest, "and his colleagues the priests who are in Jerusalem," as a document of 409 says. All the sacred personnel, the priests, Levites, singers, doorkeepers, slaves and servants of the Temple were free of tolls, tributes and customs. Here as elsewhere the Persian government favored the priesthood among its subjects as against the military aristocracy. The introduction of the

13

Torah as "the law of the Jews" by a royal decree in 445 served the same purpose. Nevertheless, it would be erroneous to regard the district of *Yehud* in the fourth century as an ecclesiastical state. While in Egypt, at the same date, a very large part of the soil belonged to the temples, and even a tithe of custom duties was assigned to them,[11] the sanctuary of Jerusalem does not appear to have possessed any real estate outside its own site, and the emoluments of the priests were offerings of the believers. Even the voluntary contribution of a third of a shekel by every male Israelite, established under Nehemiah to defray the expenses of public worship, fell into disuse.[12] But the influence of the priests continued to rise. In Nehemiah's time lay rulers of Judah led in public affairs, *e.g.*, in the dedication of the walls of Jerusalem, while the priests and the Levites purified the people; likewise plots against Nehemiah were devised among "the nobles of Judah." A century after him, a Greek traveler learned from his Jewish informant that public affairs of the Jews were administered by priests.[13]

It is a widely spread error that Judaism after Ezra was under the yoke of the Law, that the Jews were a community governed by an extreme strictness, that they were immune to foreign contagion

14

and, until the Macedonian conquest, separated from the Greek world. As a matter of fact, excavations have shown that in the fifth and fourth centuries B.C.E., Palestine belonged to the belt of an eclectic, Greco-Egyption-Asiatic culture, which extended from the Nile Delta to Cilicia.[14] The kitchen pots, as well as heavy bronze anklets worn by girls, or weapons of men, were now the same in the whole Levant, united under Persian sway. Greek painted pottery, Phoenician amulets and Egyptian idols are equally typical of Palestine in the fourth century. A Jerusalemite who went down to the coastal cities, let us say to Ascalon, could not help seeing a Greek cup showing Oedipus in conversation with the Sphinx or small bronzes of Egyptian deities. And when he returned with earthenware for his household, it might happen that he introduced into the Holy City reminiscence of a Greek mythos. An Attic black-figured cup with a sphinx has been found at Tell-En-Nashbeh, some six miles north of Jerusalem. The story, related by a pupil of Aristotle, that the master had met in Asia Minor (c. 345 B.C.E.) a Hellenized Greek-speaking Jew is probably a fiction, but not one which is improbable.[15] The commercial influence of Greece in Palestine was so great that the Athenian coins became the principal currency for trade transactions

15

in the fifth century. This currency was gradually replaced in the fourth century by local imitations of the Athenian "owls." The authorities in Palestine also struck such imitations.[16] As their small denominations show, these coins were destined for local use and for business transactions on market days. Nevertheless, used by pious Jews and even bearing the stamp of a Jewish agent of the Persian government (Hezekiah), these first Jewish coins show not only the owl of the Athenian model but also human figures,[17] and even the image of a divinity seated on a winged wheel.[18] Whether the die cutter simply imitated here the Baal of the Tarsian coins or intended to represent in this way the "Lord of Hosts," these coins are hardly in accord with the biblical interdiction of "graven images." In fact, being real men and not puppets like the characters portrayed in conventional textbooks, the Jews of the Restoration, like those of every generation, were entangled in contradictions and in conflicting patterns of real life.

They were convinced that God set them apart from the nations (Lev. 20:24), but they called Him the God of Heaven, which was the title of Ahuramazda, the deity of their Persian rulers. They regarded as Israel's heritage the whole land from Dan to Beer-sheba, even from Egypt to the Orontes

(I Chron. 13:5), but did not establish friendly relations with the remnants of Ephraim who worshiped the same God and consecrated His priests according to the prescriptions of the Torah (II Chron. 13:9). In Jerusalem in the fourth century the priesthood was considered firmly organized by David himself, but among these ancient priestly families were some like the clan Hakoz, which had been regarded as of doubtful lineage only a hundred years before. The Jews imagined that they were living according to the Law of Moses, while the synagogue, unknown to the Torah, became a fundamental part of their devotional life. So "the congregation of the Lord" became the basic element of the nation[19] and a Jerusalemite could not imagine the national kings of the past acting otherwise than in agreement with the Holy Community (I Chron. 13:1; 16:1; 28:8; 29:1; II Chron. 30:4). Of still greater significance was another innovation: how the Torah came to be taught "throughout all the cities of Judah" (II Chron. 17:9). Before this the priests had kept to themselves the decision on matters of ritual and of morals. The knowledge comes from the priest's lips, says an author of the age of Ezra and Nehemiah, and law from the priest's mouth, because he is the messenger of the Lord (Mal. 2:7). But the democratization of the instruction in the Law in the fourth century opened the way to the coming of the scribe, and imperceptibly compromised the supremacy of the priest. From now on, the superiority of learned argument over authoritative decree prevailed. The First Psalm presents as the model of happiness not the officiating priests in the Temple, but rather the Sage who meditates on the Torah day and night. Scribes and Sages, clergy and laymen, the Jews were expected to be "saints," holy unto the Lord (Lev. 20:26). But the Law of God which gave the standard of holiness was imposed upon the saints by the decree of their pagan sovereign.

Another widespread and mistaken conception is that of postexilic exclusiveness.[20] As a matter of fact, in the Persian period, the Jews were first of all peoples we know to open wide the gates to proselytes. Every ancient cult was exclusive; none but the members of a family participated in the worship of its tutelary gods; no foreigner was able to sacrifice to the deities of a city.[21] When Orestes, masked as a stranger, returns to his ancestral home, he asks permission to take part in religious ceremonies, "if strangers may sacrifice with citizens."[22] In the fifth century B.C.E. the Athenians equally assume that it is a "calamity" to have an alien father.[23] They were proud of being autochthonous, and not immigrants of mixed blood. In 333 B.C.E., when Alexander the Great was already making war in Asia, a special law was necessary in Athens to authorize the shrine of a foreign deity on the sacred soil of Pallas.[24] But the Jewish law allowed a stranger sojourning among the Jews to keep the Passover with the congregation of Israel (Ezra 6:21). "One law shall be to him that is homeborn, and unto the stranger who sojourns among you" (Ex. 12:49). And again: "The stranger who sojourns with you shall be to you as the homeborn among you, and thou shalt love him as thyself" (Lev. 19:34). An Athenian contemporary of Ezra would be astonished to hear that he has to love the *Metoeci*. Equally startling for the ancient world was the idea of proselytism, the appeal to the nations to join themselves to the Lord, which began with Second Isaiah and was repeated by later prophets again and again. "Thus says the Lord of hosts: In those days it shall come to pass, that ten men shall take hold, out of all the languages of the nations, shall even take hold of the skirt of him that is a Jew, saying: We will go with you, for we have heard that God is with you" (Zech. 8:23). So, the postexilic community establishes the new and really revolutionary principle: "Thus says the

19

Lord: My house shall be called a house of prayer for all peoples" (Is. 56:7).

Again we meet with the fact that every historical situation is many-sided and full of contradictions. The heathens were tolerant and their gods lived amicably side by side because each nation had its own gods who did not care for other people. An Argive refugee in Athens is told not to be afraid of the Argive gods: "We have gods who fight on our side and who are not weaker than those on the side of the Argives."[25] Thus, the pagans made no efforts to convert a stranger but, for the same reason, excluded him from their own religion. Everybody was a true believer, in the opinion of the heathen, if he worshiped his ancestral gods. Thus, each city was exclusive and intolerant within its walls, but recognized the other gods outside. On the other hand, knowing that the Lord is the One True God, the Jews naturally proselytized among the heathen and admitted the converted to the universal religion. And for that same reason they were intolerant of those outside the congregation and rejected the folly of idolatry. Only a Jew was a true believer, but everybody could enter the congregation of the Chosen People.

The thought of this period is illustrated in an anonymous historical composition which now appears in the Bible as Ezra-Nehemiah and Chronicles. The arrangement reveals that the latter part of the orginal work (Ezra-Nehemiah) found its way into the scriptural canon before the portion (Chronicles) which related the pre-exilic history already covered by the Books of Samuel and Kings. But the work originally formed a single, continuous narrative from Adam to Nehemiah; it was still read in this edition by the compiler of a Greek version (the so-called First Esdras) in the second century B.C.E.

For the pre-exilic period the Chronicler draws for the most part on the Books of Samuel and Kings, but adds a great deal of information from other sources. Historians usually discount this additional material and blame the Chronicler for his little regard for facts. He can, for instance, state coolly that David had 1,570,000 warriors, exclusive of the troops of Levi and Benjamin (I Chron. 21:5). But the same exuberance in numbers is displayed by Assyrian records, and the source of the Chronicler (II Sam. 24) gives a number no less fantastic for David's army: 1,300,000. Fact-hunting critics overlook a very important feature of the work: its emancipation from the authority of tradition.

Oriental historiography is strictly traditional. An

Assyrian reviser of royal annals may transform a booty of 1,235 sheep into one of 100,225,[26] or attribute to the king a successful campaign of his predecessor; but in the main he simply summarizes his source. The compiler of Kings closely follows his authorities, although he adds personal comments to the events. The Chronicler, like Hecataeus of Miletus or Herodotus, gives such information concerning the past as appears to him most probable, and corrects the sources in conformity with his own historical standards. For instance, when he asserts that the Levites carried the Ark in accordance with David's order (I Chron. 15:1), he interpolates something into his source (II Sam. 6:12) because he assumes as self-evident that the pious king could not but act according to the Law of Moses (Ex. 25:13). For the same reason he says "Levites" (II Chron. 5:4) when his source (I Kings 8:3) speaks of "priests" taking up the Ark under Solomon. Following his rule of historical probability, he cannot believe that Solomon turned over some cities to Hiram of Tyre (I Kings 9:12); so he changes the text: the cities were given by Hiram to Solomon (II Chron. 8:2). In the same manner, he attributes to ancient kings, David and Josiah, the organization of the priesthood and of the sacred services as they existed in his own time. Since Israel had ceased to be an independent state, the author treats with predilection all matters concerning the Temple, which now became the center of national life, and devotes a long description to religious measures of King Hezekiah which are hardly mentioned in Kings. Owing to the shift of historical interest, he passes over in silence the Northern Kingdom, which had rebelled against the house of David. He does not hesitate to use the term "Israel" when he speaks of Judah, which alone remained faithful to the covenant of the fathers.

The critics have often stressed the Chronicler's practice of viewing the past as the realization in Israel of the rules and principles of the Torah, his tendency to find the origins of the Judaism of his own day in remote antiquity. In fact, his purpose is not to give a mere chronicle but to provide a clue to the meaning and direction of Israel's history. The same attempt, with regard to Greek (and even world) history, was made by Herodotus, who wrote about a hundred years before the Chronicler. Herodotus seems to feel that the gods, envious of human greatness and happiness, use man's wrongdoings to punish him or his posterity. It is the doctrine of Nemesis, exemplified, for instance, in Polycrates's fate. The moral of history is, therefore, to remain an average man; its lesson is that of moderation and submission to destiny, the "nothing in excess" of the Seven Sages.

The Jewish author finds in divine pragmatism the principle for understanding the past; his clue is the idea of retribution. That is, of course, nothing new. Herodotus explains Croesus' fall by the sin of his ancestor in the fifth generation. In a cuneiform text Nabonidus's evil-doing explains his fall and the catastrophe of Babylon.[27] But the Chronicler describes the whole of human history from this standpoint. According to his conception, the pious kings always enjoyed prosperity, while punishment necessarily befell the wicked and unfaithful ones. The idea is applied to the reinterpretation of the past with the same constancy and disregard of facts as when some modern books describe history in terms of class struggle or racial changes. From Saul to the last king, Zedekiah, the evil-doers die for their transgressions. But, since the Chronicler conceives of Divine Necessity in human history as the work of the personal God and not of a machinelike Fate of the Greeks, he seeks to justify the visitations sent upon Israel. In the first place, he stresses the idea of personal responsibility. He follows and repeats (II Chron. 25:4) the principle established in Deuteronomy (24:16) that "the fathers shall not be put to death for the children, neither shall the children be put to death for the fathers; every man shall be put to death for his own sin," a conception which appears about the same time in Greece too. But the principle of collective responsibility remained active in Greece, except for Athens, with regard to political crimes.[28] In Judaism, the Book of Kings still presents the hand of God visiting the sins of the fathers upon their children and striking peoples for the transgressions of their kings. Jehoiachin is carried away and Judah is destroyed in 597 "for the sins of Manasseh" who had reigned almost fifty years before (II Kings 24:3; Jer. 15:4). The Chronicler assumes that Manasseh had received a due punishment from the Assyrians, who led him about in fetters and held on to him by a hook thrust into his nostrils (II Chron. 33:11). On the other hand, the destruction of Jerusalem in 587 is explained in Kings (II Kings 24:20) as an expression of God's anger against the last king, Zedekiah. The Chronicler adds that "all the chiefs of the priests, and the people, trangressed very greatly after all the abominations of the nations; and they polluted the house of the Lord which He had hallowed in Jerusalem" (II Chron. 36:14). The Syrian invasion in the reign of Joash is a judgment on the people, "because they had forsaken the Lord, the God of their fathers" (II Chron. 24:24).

The invasion of Shishak happened because all Israel had transgressed along with King Rehoboam (II Chron. 12:1). Consequently, the deliverance from Sennacherib is caused by the reconciliation of the people with God, and the author is fond of associating the people with the king in religious reformations (I Chron. 13:4; II Chron. 30:4f.).

This conception of personal responsibility for transgression explains the role of the prophets in Chronicles. Herodotus uses the Oriental theme of the wise counselor to show how man in his blindness neglects prudent advice and runs to his doom. The Chronicler knows that God sent His prophets "because He had compassion on His people" (II Chron. 36:15); but they mocked His messengers and despised His words. So the culprit was fully conscious of the culpability of his deed and duly warned, a proviso which later talmudic jurisprudence requires for legal conviction and punishment of a capital offender. Thus, warned by God, the wicked kings sinned with malice and God's wrath was fully justified. Accordingly, the Chronicler's standard in judging the ancient kings is their obedience to the Divine Message sent through the prophets. Jerusalem was destroyed because Israel scoffed at the warnings of the prophets. The Temple was rebuilt by Cyrus, in order that the Word of the

Lord by the mouth of Jeremiah might be accomplished (II Chron. 36:22). This, "the Chronicle of the whole of sacred history," as Jerome calls it, leads to the Restoration under Persian rule. When the adversaries of Jerusalem frustrate the building of the Temple, King Darius intervenes, and the Jews dedicate the sanctuary and prosper "through the prophesying of Haggai . . . and Zechariah" (Ezra 6:14).

In keeping with ancient historiography, the recital becomes fuller when the compiler approaches his own time. But some features of the latter part of his work are peculiar. In the first place, we note that while the author considers Nehemiah's days as being in the past (Neh. 12:47), he does not continue the narrative until his own time but ends with the account of Nehemiah's measures which concluded the Restoration in 432 B.C.E. In the same way, Herodotus (and other Greek historians in the fifth century) did not deal with the events after the Persian wars.[29] Again, while for the pre-exilic period the Chronicler refers to many sources, for the Persian epoch he gives hardly anything other than a reproduction of official records: lists, letters and memoranda of royal administration, memorials of Ezra and of Nehemiah. He scarcely provides notes of his own for a chronological and logical framework. And, while he freely passes judgment on ancient persons and times, he refrains from expressing his personal views in the account of the Persian period. One is reminded of Greek *logographi* of the fifth century who, as an ancient critic says, repeated "the written records that they found preserved in temples or secular buildings in the form in which they found them, neither adding nor taking away anything."[30]

This dependence on source material leads, quite naturally, to some confusion. As the Chronicler confuses, for instance, Darius I with Darius II, he places a dossier referring to Xerxes and Artaxerxes I before their predecessor Darius I. The Chronicler quotes Ezra's and Nehemiah's accounts in their own words, a feature which involved the change from the third person to the first person and *vice versa.* This device served to authenticate the narrative and came into historical writing from the diplomatic style, where exactness of quotation was absolutely necessary. In Egypt the story of the war of King Kamose in the sixteenth century B.C.E., or the epic of the victory of Rameses II at Kadesh, *c.* 1300 B.C.E., presents the same change from a subjective account to objective praise by the hero of his own deeds.[31] The so-called "Letters to God Assur" in Assyrian historiography likewise show the use of the third person when the king is spoken of in the introduction composed by a scribe, while in the body of the text the king speaks in the first person.[32] In a Persian tract composed after the conquest of Babylon in 538 B.C.E., the so-called Cyrus cylinder, the author relates the evil-doings of Nabonidus, the last king of Babylon, and the conquest of the city by Cyrus. Then, without any transition, exactly as in Ezra-Nehemiah, the author introduces Cyrus's proclamation, beginning "I am Cyrus," which gives Cyrus's own account of the events.[33] When the Chronicler quotes documents verbatim, he again follows the style of chancelleries. He introduces even in his narratives of pre-exilic history such compositions couched in official form, e.g., a circular communication of King Hezekiah (II Chron. 30) and even a letter of the prophet Elijah (II Chron. 21:12).[34]

Ezra's and Nehemiah's prayers, the national confession of sins, the covenants made with God under the leadership of Ezra and Nehemiah are presented as proof that there is a difference between the wicked Jerusalem of the kings and the new Israel which decided to follow the way of righteousness. That accounts for the blessing of the present state under the protection of the Persian kings. The Temple is restored "according to the commandment of the God of Israel, and according to the decree of Cyrus, and Darius; and Artaxerxes king of Persia" (Ezra 6:14).

The whole conception of the Chronicler shows that he wrote when Persian rule seemed destined for eternity and the union between the altar in Jerusalem and the throne of Susa seemed to be natural and indestructible. The Chronicler wrote before Alexander the Great, that is, in the first half of the fourth century. Accordingly, the tendency of his work is to recommend a kind of political quietism which should please the court of Susa as well as the High Priest's mansion in Jerusalem. The idea of the Messianic age which was destined to come after the overthrow of the Persian world power, finds no place in the work of the Chronicler. Armies are superfluous for Israel, the Jews need not fight when the Lord is with them; the Chronicler does not tire of stressing this conception. But "the Lord is with you while you are with Him" (II Chron. 15:2). Zedekiah was punished and Jerusalem destroyed not only because the king did evil and did not give heed to Jeremiah's words, but also because "he rebelled against King Nebuchadnezzar, who had made him swear by God." That is taken from Ezekiel (17:13) but the lesson could

30

hardly escape the attention of the Chronicler's readers, subjects of the Persian king.

The Chronicler's historical work, Attic pottery unearthed in Palestine, Jewish coins bearing a Divine Image, universalism and exclusiveness, all these together create a picture of Jewish life after the Restoration rather different from what is conveyed by the conventional cliches. They indicate that life was more vivid, more diversified than the rules of conduct as formulated in Scripture might suggest.

———

A postexilic oracle included in the Book of Isaiah (11:11) promises the return of the Diaspora from Elam, Assyria, Babylonia, Lower and Upper Egypt, from North Syria and "from the islands of the sea." This Jewish Diaspora encountered everywhere the Hellenic Diaspora. Greek trading stations existed in the fifth and fourth centuries, for example, at Ugarit (near modern Lattakie) and at the mouth of the Orontes in Syria.[35] When in 586 Jewish refugees from Palestine, Jeremiah among them, went to "Tahpanhes" in the Egyptian Delta, they entered a settlement of Greek mercenaries, established here (Daphne) by Psammetichus.[36] Payments of rations listed in a Babylonian account between 595 and 570 B.C.E. were provided not only to King Joiachin [Jehoiachin] and numerous other men of Judah in exile, but also to Ionian carpenters and shipbuilders.[37] As cuneiform business documents of the Persian period show, the Jews in the Babylonian Diaspora rubbed shoulders with men from India and Armenia and Turkestan and, of course, Lydians and Ionians.[38] When later Greek authors supposed that Pythagoras, that ancient sage of Samos, was indebted not only to Egypt and Chaldea, but to Jewish wisdom, too, when a later Jewish author thought that the Greek sages had learned loftier conceptions of God from Moses, they were probably wrong, but the surmise does not any longer appear absurd in the light of recent discoveries. One may fancy Ezekiel talking with Pythagoras in Babylon; they speak of Homer and of Moses. What a topic for an *Imaginary Conversation* in Landor's fashion!

But our information concerning the Diaspora in the Persian period is scanty and accidental. To be sure, we still have numerous records from Babylonia, written between 464 and 404 B.C.E., with many Jewish names.[39] But since these tablets are business documents of one pagan firm in Nippur, in southern Babylonia, we do not really learn anything substantial of the life of the Jews from these contracts and receipts. Nevertheless, these archives show that the *golah* of 597 and 587 still remained on the same place where the exiled had been settled by Nebuchadnezzar, namely, "by the river Chebar" (Ez. 1:1), which is the "large canal" of the cuneiform tablets, a watercourse on which Nippur was situated. The Jews in the documents often bear Babylonian and Persian names, some of them combined with the names of pagan deities. For instance, the father of a Hanana is called Ardi-Gula, that is, "servant of [the Goddess] Gula." But about seventy per cent of the Jews had genuine Hebrew names. The Jews in the district of Nippur were for the most part farmers; but they were also tax collectors and royal officials; they held military tenures and transacted business with the Babylonians and the Persians. A Jewish claimant opposes a Babylonian merchant house "in the judicial assembly of Nippur."

There were many Jewish settlements in Egypt, too; for instance, in the Delta, near Pelusium, at Memphis, and in upper Egypt. The Egyptian Diaspora was pre-exilic. Even before the Exile an oracle signifies five cities in the land of Egypt that speak the language of Canaan and swear to the Lord of Hosts (Is. 19:18), and the Second Isaiah (49:12) mentions the Jews in the land of Sinim, that is, Syene, at the first cataract of the Nile, at the southern border of Egypt. To this place Jewish mercenaries were sent by one of their kings in the beginning of the sixth century to help the Pharaoh. Guardian of the Ethiopian boundary, "the Jewish force" came into Persian service after Cambyses' conquest of Egypt (525 B.C.E.), and obeyed the

34

Pharaohs again after the defection of Egypt in 404. Numerous documents in Aramaic of the fifth century, belonging to this military settlement, have been unearthed at Elephantine.[40]

The "Jewish force" (as the regiment is officially styled) was divided into companies, the captains of which bear Babylonian or Persian names; a Persian was "the chief of the force." The settlers received pay and rations (barley, lentils, etc.) from the royal treasury. But the colony was civilian in its way of life. The Jews at Elephantine bought and sold their tenures, transacted business, defended their claims in civil courts, although everyone, even women, was styled as belonging to the regiment. The Jews dealt with military colonists of other nations settled in the neighborhood, as well as with Egyptians. There were mixed marriages. Independently of the military organization the Jews formed a religious community of the kind later, in the Hellenistic period, called *politeuma*. A president "with his colleagues" represented the community which was gathered in "assembly" whenever wanted. The president was also the treasurer of the local Temple of the national God, whom these Jews called "Yahu" and regarded as "the God of Heaven." Likewise, their system of sacrifices and the terms referring to them were the same as in the Bible: holocaust, meal offering, incense; they offered libations and immolated sheep, oxen and goats. They observed the Passover. Their faith was rather homely and plain. They suggested in a letter that their enemy was killed, "and the dogs tore off the anklets from his legs," because they had prayed for it to the God of Heaven and fasted "with our wives and our children" in sackcloth. They did not doubt that merit before God may be obtained with expensive sacrifices, and would hardly appreciate the prophetic word that God desires mercy and not sacrifices (Hos. 6:6). But equally, they did not suspect that their place of worship was a violation of Divine Law proclaimed in Deuteronomy, which forbids altars and immolations outside of the one chosen place at Jerusalem. With the same "provincial" naïveté, they uttered blessings in the name of "Yahu and Khnum."

While the religion of the Jews of Elephantine was primitive their business activity was highly modern. They wrote, and probably talked, not Hebrew but Aramaic, which had become the common and official language of the Persian Empire. Accordingly, while contemporary demotic documents reflect Egyptian law, and while Mesopotamian settlers near Aleppo (Syria) and at Gezer (Palestine) continued to draw cuneiform deeds in harmony with the Babylonian system,[41] the Aramaic records from Elephantine manifest the formation and development of a new common law of the Levant. The form of these instruments is that of a declaration made before witnesses and reproduced in direct speech; this is modeled on Egyptian formularies. The same form is used in an Aramaic lease agreement of 515 B.C.E. entered into in Egypt by two parties not of Jewish origin. Some stipulations in business documents from Elephantine reproduce Egyptian formulae also, *e.g.*, the abandonment of the claims to a ceded property. But the term "hate" for separation of spouses is Babylonian and biblical (Deut. 21:15), although it was also borrowed by the Egyptians. Babylonian too are the contracts of renunciation arising from a previous decision of the court, the legal term for "instituting a suit" and the standard of weight. This syncretistic common law was built up partly by precedents set by the Persian king's judges, partly by way of customary agreements. The Persian court adopted, for instance, the Egyptian practice of imposing an oath (formulated by the judge) upon the party in support of the claim when there was no other evidence, even when the litigants were of different nationalities, *e.g.*, a Jew and a Persian. Everybody was required, of course, to swear by his

37

own deity; when a Jewess became the wife of an Egyptian, she was supposed to follow the status of her husband and she took oath by an Egyptian goddess. On the other hand, polygamy, allowed in Jewish law, was prohibited in marriage contracts of Elephantine by a stipulation agreed upon by the parties and guaranteed by a fine. While Egyptian marriage was based on mere consensus, the Jews at Elephantine still regarded a union as valid only when the bride's father received from the groom a "marriage price" *(mohar)*. But this conveyance of rights to the husband became here an antiquated formality. The new common law established an almost complete equality between spouses. Both had the right to divorce at his or her pleasure, provided the declaration of "hating" was made "in the congregation." The power to divorce was given to the bride in Egyptian marriage contracts, but it was limited to the husband alone in Jewish (and Babylonian) law. Egyptian too was the status of woman with regard to her legal capacity; married or not, she was able at Elephantine to conduct business, hold property in her own right and resort to law about it. No less surprising was the stipulation that either spouse would inherit from the other when there were no children. Thus, the Aramaic papyri from Elephantine of the fifth century B.C.E. are the earliest evidence we have for the transformation of the Jewish behavior in the Dispersion. Living on equal terms with the natives, transacting business with peoples of various races, intermarrying, the Diaspora began to diverge from the course followed at Jerusalem.

But living together with other people rarely continues untroubled. Although the priest of the Egyptian god Khnum was a neighbor of the Jewish sanctuary at Elephantine for many decades, in 411 the Egyptian clergy bribed the Persian governor to order the Jewish temple destroyed. One may doubt whether that was really "the first anti-Semitic outbreak," as the action is now considered by historians. When we read the endless complaints of a certain Peteesi, an Egyptian (513 B.C.E.), about vexations he was forced to suffer from Egyptian priests on account of some litigation,[42] we are rather prepared to believe that the conflict of 411 at Elephantine was a local incident, and not a symptom of general anti-Semitism. When the Persian governor refused to allow the reconstruction of the temple, the Jews of Elephantine sent an appeal to Jerusalem. But the existence of a temple outside Zion could hardly please the authorities at Jerusalem. Consequently, in 408, the Jews of Elephantine wrote to Bagoas, the Persian governor of

Judea, and to the sons of Sanballat, governor of Samaria, hinting also at a forthcoming bribe. The addressees prepared a memorandum recommending to the satrap of Egypt the reestablishment of the temple, without animal offerings, however: a compromise which would please both the Egyptians, who at this time worshiped almost every animal, and the Jerusalemites, who in this manner reduced the altar of Elephantine to a lower rank.

But there were again intrigues and counterintrigues, bribes and favors at the court of the Persian satrap of Egypt; and since, toward the end of the fifth century, Egypt rebelled against Persia, the temple at Elephantine was never rebuilt, although the Jewish military settlement continued and was ultimately taken over by Alexander the Great.

THE POLICIES OF

ALEXANDER THE GREAT

———

The Persian Empire fell in 333. When Alexander the Great proceeded down the coast of Syria toward Egypt, most peoples and cities on his route, Jerusalem among them, readily submitted to the Macedonian. The meeting of Jewish deputies, sent to offer the surrender of the Holy City, with the world conqueror later became a choice topic of Jewish legend. In fact, the Macedonian, who considered himself the legitimate heir of the Persian kings, here as elsewhere simply accepted and confirmed the statutes and privileges granted by his Iranian predecessors. But an accidental order of Alexander's deeply influenced the history of Palestine.

The city of Samaria revolted in 332, and the king, having taken it, settled Macedonians there. This punishment, inflicted on Samaria, brought about the break between Judah and Ephraim. Captured by the Assyrians in 722, the city of

Samaria had become a military colony. The men from Babylonia and northern Syria transplanted here, brought along their own gods, such as the god of pestilence, Nergal of Cutha, who at the same time appeared in Sidon, a city also resettled by the Assyrians after the rebellion of 677. Being polytheists, the settlers in due course adopted the deity of the land in which they dwelt and learned to worship the God of Israel with great zeal. Since Sargon in 722 deported only the higher classes of the district of Samaria, the countryside was not denuded of the original population. Sargon himself refers to the tribute imposed on this remnant of Israel.

The newcomers intermingled and intermarried with the former inhabitants of the land of Samaria and accepted their religion. In 586, men of Shiloh and Samaria came and worshiped at the ruined site of the Temple of Jerusalem. In 520 the Samaritans claimed a share in the rebuilding of this Temple. As already noted, in 408 the Jews at Elephantine wrote to the leaders in both Jerusalem and Samaria as to coreligionists. Still later there were people of Ephraim who celebrated the Passover at Jerusalem (II Chron. 34:6). It seems that the conversion of the heathen immigrants to the service of the God of Israel was complete and that both Samaria and Jerusalem worshiped the same God with the same rites in the fourth century B.C.E. There is no mention of any pagan cult among the Samaritans. Accordingly, prophets in Jerusalem expected the redemption of both "prisoners of hope" (Zech. 9:13), Judah and Ephraim. The conflict between the two cities under Persian rule was primarily a political one. Samaria opposed the rebuilding of the walls of Jerusalem because the resurrected capital in the south would be a natural rival of the northern fortress. In the same way, the Assyrian settlers in Sidon, who became completely assimilated with the natives, inherited their quarrel with Tyre, another Phoenician capital.

But when Alexander planted Macedonian colonists in the city of Samaria, he destroyed the fusion between "the force at Samaria" and the countryside. The new masters of the stronghold did not know anything about the God of Israel. They did not care for Nergal either. They were at home rather in Athens, where in the third century B.C.E. a pagan association crowned a certain "Samaritan" as its benefactor. If the new inhabitants were inclined to adopt some elements of the religion of the former settlers, they could hardly succeed because the God of Israel did not tolerate any rival.

It often happened that when a Greek colony was established, native villages under its control formed a union around an ancestral sanctuary. Following the same pattern, the countryside of (now Macedonian) Samaria constituted an organization, in Greek style, "Sidonians of Shechem," for the purpose of serving the God of Israel.[43] Shechem, the most ancient capital and the most sacred site of Israel, became the natural center of the confederation. The name "Sidonians," that is, "Canaanites," was probably chosen in opposition to the newcomers; it emphasized the fact that the members of the League were aboriginal inhabitants of Canaan. The geographical term "Samaritans" was appropriated by the Macedonian intruders, and the religious term "Israel" now belonged to Jerusalem. The descendants of the Assyrian settlers, men like Sanballat, Nehemiah's adversary, who had been the leaders in Palestine for four centuries and who were now dispossessed, could neither accept the predominance of the Macedonian colony nor become a dependency of Jerusalem. They repeated to the Jews, "we seek your God as you do" (Ezra 4:2), but were not prepared to recognize the demands of Jerusalem that the common Deity may not be rightfully worshiped away from the summit of Zion. As the Chronicler emphasized (II Chron. 30:10), such claims were received with derision in the north.

The new union around Shechem, therefore, founded its own sanctuary. It was consecrated to the God of both Jerusalem and Shechem, and stood on the summit of Gerizim, overlooking Shechem, on the site where the Chosen People were commanded to "set the blessing," according to the precept of Deuteronomy (11:29). Deuteronomy was originally a Jerusalemite book, published in 621 B.C.E., but since 722 B.C.E. there had been no center of the religion of the fathers outside Jerusalem, and the worshipers of God, in Samaria or elsewhere, had to seek guidance at Jerusalem. The choice of Gerizim shows the dependence of the Shechemites on Jerusalem in spiritual matters and, at the same time, it proves that only the pride of the former Assyrian aristocrats, loath to acknowledge the supremacy of the southern rival, was responsible for the foundation of the Samaritan temple, and, consequently, for the break between Judah and Ephraim. The whole controversy between Jews and Samaritans was now subordinated to the question: Which place was chosen by God for His inhabitation, Zion or Gerizim? Later propagandist inventions obscured the origin of the schism and confused its dating which, for this reason, remains controversial. The Samaritans glorified their temple by attributing its founding to Alexander the Great. The Jews associated the separation with Nehemiah's expulsion of a scion of the high-priestly family for his marriage to a Samaritan girl (Neh. 13:28). This combination provided a "rational" account for the schism, and conveniently branded the priesthood at Gerizim as illegitimate. But the Jewish tradition itself, repeated by Josephus, states that the Samaritan temple was founded at the time of Alexander the Great. The fact that it did not receive any subvention from the Macedonian rulers, as well as the fact that it belonged not to Samaria but to "that foolish nation which dwells in Shechem" (as Ben Sira says), offers the definitive proof of its foundation after the Macedonian conquest.

Jerusalem was situated far away from the main trade routes which crossed Palestine and ran along the coast. Thus, while the Greeks knew the Palestinian shore very well, no Greek writer before the time of Alexander the Great mentions the Jews, with the exception of Herodotus, who alludes to the circumcision practiced by "the Phoenicians and the Syrians of Palestine." But even after Alexander the Great, the first Greek authors who took cognizance of the Jews got their information from the Diaspora, from Jewish immigrants or Jewish soldiers in the service of Alexander and his successors. That is by no mean surprising. Why should a Greek author, at a time when the whole fabulous Orient was open to his inquiry, concentrate on a Lilliputian place in the arid mountains? Let us note, by the way, that the first Greek book (by Aristotle's pupil Theophrastus) giving some exact information about Rome, appeared in 314-313 B.C.E. Some years later another student of philosophy, Hecataeus of Abdera, who had accompanied Ptolemy I of Egypt in his Syrian campaign of 312 B.C.E., published in a report of his journey the first Greek account of the Jews, based particularly on data given to the author by a Jewish priest who, in 312, accompanied the Ptolemaic army to Egypt.[44] Hecataeus's narrative was used by Theophrastus,[45] while another pupil of Aristotle, Clearchus, described what is probably a fictitious meeting between his master and a Jewish magician in Asia Minor.[46]

Let us consider the picture of the Jews as seen with Greek eyes at the end of the fourth century. For the reason just stated, a Greek writer must have had a particular motive to take an interest in the Jews. Now, the philosophers, and the school of Aristotle in particular, looked for empirical confirmation of their social theories in the newly opened Orient. Similarly, the discovery of America was utilized by European scholars of the sixteenth

century to identify the Red Indians with the los
Ten Tribes. Greek scholars of Alexander's time
thought that the peoples untouched by the dis-
solving influence of modern (that is, Greek) civilization must have conserved the purity of religion
and the perfection of social organization which the
philosophers attributed to man in a state of nature.
On the other hand, the Greeks knew that in the
Orient knowledge was the monopoly of the priestly
caste. Having discovered a people led by priests and
obeying the Law coming directly from the Divinity,
the Greeks ranged the Jews beside the Indian Brah-
mans and Persian Magi. The Jews are a "philosophical race," says Theophrastus; they descend from the
Indian philosophers, says Clearchus. Just as a Greek
author (Megasthenes) claimed that the doctrines of
the ancient Greek philosophers concerning nature
had been formulated by the Indians, other writers
ascribed the origins of philosophy to the Jews.
Clearchus presents a Jewish sage who furnishes
Aristotle with the experimental proof of the Platonic doctrine of immortality. Some decades later,
Hermippus, another follower of Aristotle, mentions
the (supposed) Jewish belief in the soul's immortality as a well-known fact, and adds that
Pythagoras borrowed from the Jews and the Thracians his opinions about it. Since the Jews named

their Deity "God of Heaven," they provided the philosophers with the desired proof that natural theology of mankind had identified God with the heavens. Likewise, monotheism, as well as the absence of divine images, agreed with the philosophical conceptions. Other data was interpreted accordingly. For instance, Theophrastus states that the Jews celebrate their festivals at night in contemplation of the stars (the order of heavenly bodies was for the philosophers the most important proof against atheism) and discourse about the Divine. In the same way, Hecataeus ascribes to the Egyptian priests philosophical conversations during the banquets where wine was not served.

The political organization of the Jews was viewed from the same standpoint, as the realization of an ideal state, governed by the Sages, the philosophers according to Plato and the priests according to the Palestinians. The Torah is presented as a narrative of the settlement of the Jews in Palestine and as their constitution. Moses, as lawgiver, could establish his system only after the conquest; so, according to Hecataeus, he had conquered the Promised Land and founded Jerusalem. As in Sparta, his system is based on military virtues of bravery, endurance and discipline. As is fit for the perfect state, the legislator forbade the sale of the land distributed among the Jews of Palestine in order to prevent the concentration of wealth and its sinister consequence, the decrease of population. This Greek interpretation of Lev. 25:23 clearly shows that Hecataeus's inquiry was oriented by his philosophic aims; he elicited from his Jewish informants answers which could serve his theory. For this reason it is a very delicate task to appreciate the earliest Greek records as testimony regarding the state of Judaism in Alexander's time. When Hecataeus affirms that the priests receive a tithe of the income of the people, he idealizes the realities. When he adds that the priests administer public affairs, he surely gives a one-sided view of the subject. But when he emphatically states that the High Priest was regarded as the mouthpiece of God and messenger of divine oracles, we suspect that the Greek writer attributes to the Jews the behavior they should have in his opinion, in order to represent the ideal scheme of the philosophical commonwealth. Hecataeus's High Priest, by the way, is chosen as the most able leader among the priests.

Some features stressed in the Greek records are worth noting. The importance of the priesthood and the role of the High Priest in Jerusalem, the obstinacy of the Jews in defense of the Law and the slander of their neighbors and foreign visitors with regard to antialien sentiments of the Jews, already point in Hecataeus's narrative to characteristic features of Hellenistic Jewry. We learn that already before 300 B.C.E. the Jews in Palestine did not tolerate pagan shrines and altars on the holy soil and that, at the same time, the Jews in the Diaspora freely scoffed at the superstitions of the Gentiles. This attitude was inevitable because the Jews were in possession of the Truth. They might have said to the pagans: We claim liberty for ourselves in accordance with your principles and refuse it to you in accordance with our principles. In the polytheist world of Hellenism, where all beliefs were admitted as different refractions of the same eternal light, the Jewish claim to the oneness of the Divine Revelation must have appeared as a provocation.

Nevertheless, Alexander and his successors accepted the Jews among the citizens of the new settlements founded in the East. When the experiment of founding commonwealths of Greek type in the Orient succeeded, later descendants of the settlers became "Aristocrats" but the first settlers were no more respected by their contemporaries than the passengers of the *Mayflower* were by the Englishmen of 1620. The conquest of Alexander, welding East and West into a single economic whole, brought wealth to Greece and to many Oriental towns. Why should a craftsman from Athens or a moneylender from Babylon enroll in the list of settlers of a new city far away, let us say Europos on the Euphrates? As the kings needed cities to safeguard the military communications and as strongholds against the indigenous population, settlers were at a premium. For instance, Alexander transferred some contingents from (still Assyrian) Samaria to Egypt, where they received allotments of land. There is no reason to suspect Josephus's statement that the early Hellenistic rulers gave the Jews equal status with the Macedonians and Greeks who settled in the new colonies. He fails to make it clear that these privileges were individual and did not bear on the position of Jewry as a community in the new colony. This was a point on which hinged the later struggle between the Greeks and the Jews in Hellenistic cities. We do not know how Alexander and his successors reconciled Jewish exclusiveness with the obligations of the Greek citizen. Probably, the antinomy was solved in each case empirically. There were Jews, like the magician spoken of by Clearchus, who "not only spoke Greek, but had the soul of a Greek," and thus were inclined to mutual tolerance. Sometimes the king exempted the Jews; thus Alexander pardoned the Jewish soldiers who had refused to build a heathen temple in Babylon, and Seleucus I ordered money to be given for oil to those Jews, citizens of Antiochia, who were unwilling to use pagan oil. As oil was given by the "gymnasiarchs" for anointing during athletic games, the notice seems to imply that in Greek cities of the Diaspora, Jewish youth about 300 B.C.E. already took part in exercises of the "gymnasia," naked like their Hellenic comrades.[47] Physical training was the foundation of Greek life and mentality in all Greek cities, and the gymnasia became the centers of Greek intellectual activity and the principal instrument of Hellenization. Through the palaestra, by way of sports, the Jewish settlers became recognized members of the community. They learned to take pride in the city long before Paul proclaimed at Jerusalem his double title of honor, "I am a Jew, a Tarsian of Cilicia, citizen of no mean city." And conversely, the Jews of Alexandria could not but imagine that Alexander had become a worshiper of the true God at the time of his founding of their city and had brought the bones of the prophet Jeremiah to Alexandria as her palladium.[48]

After Alexander's death (324 B.C.E.) wars between his generals ended in the dismemberment of his empire. After 301 there were three great powers governed by Macedonian dynasties: Asia (that is substantially Syria, Mesopotamia, Persia and a large portion of Asia Minor) under the sway of the Seleucids, Egypt of the Ptolemies, and the realm of Macedonia in Europe. Thus, the political unity of the world where the Jews lived was broken. Even the Roman Empire did not re-establish the lost oneness, since an important Jewry remained in the Parthian kingdom, outside the laws of the Caesars.

Palestine became a dominion of Egypt but was reconquered by Antiochus III of Asia in 200 B.C.E. Since the government of both the Ptolemies and the Seleucids rested on the same political principles, we may view as an entity the period of Ptolemaic and Seleucid domination over Jerusalem until the Maccabean struggle, that is, some 125 years between 301 and 175 B.C.E. The district of Judea, called "the nation of Jews," under the Seleucids, was still a very small part of the province of Syria.[49] When a traveler passed the Jordan or the town of Modein in the north, or went south beyond Beth-zur, or toward the west descended into the coastal plain, he left the Jewish territory. Frontier guards, for instance, at Antipatris, customhouses, custom duties for export and import reminded the Jeru-salemite of this fact. Thus, even in Palestine, the political term "Jew" did not include all the re-ligious adherents of the Temple on Zion. With respect to religion there were many Jews and Jewries elsewhere, in Galilee or in Trans-Jordan or, for instance, where the powerful clan of the Tobiads was located. But politically these were not considered "Jews." The term "Jew" applied only to those "who lived around the Temple of Jeru-salem," and so a Greek historian calls them.[50] Jeru-salem was the only "city" of the Jews; other settlements in Judea were politically "villages." Judea continued to be a self-governing unit; there was no royal governor in Jerusalem, although the citadel of the Holy City was garrisoned by royal troops. The Jews, too, had to furnish contingents to the royal forces; Jewish soldiers are mentioned in Alexander's army, a Jewish regiment of cavalry under Ptolemy. It may be that fortresses on the frontier, such as that at Beth-zur, excavated recently, were occupied by native forces; about 200 B.C.E. the walls of Jerusalem were rebuilt by the Jewish authorities.

In 200 the Jewish militia helped Antiochus III to dislodge the Egyptian garrison from the citadel of Jerusalem. But more important for the central government was the collection of taxes, such as the poll tax, or taxes on houses or gate tolls, etc., to which was added the tribute, that is, the annual payment of a lump sum by the Jewish commonwealth as such. In the third century Judea, as a province of the Egyptian Empire, was part of the highly complicated system of planned economy that was built up by the Ptolemies. Like all natives of the province, "Syria and Phoenicia," the Jews had to declare their movable property and cattle for the purpose of taxation. Likewise, the Ptolemies introduced their subtle system of collecting the revenue by tax farmers. The Ptolemies favored the local notables as farmers of revenue, since in this way the native aristocracy had a stake in the Ptolemaic domination.

As regards self-government, Jerusalem was an "aristocratic" commonwealth. The "council of Elders" was the ruling body, composed of laymen and priests. But the aristocracy as a social class was priestly, just as in Hellenistic Egypt. When Antiochus III granted exemption from personal taxes to the upper class in Jerusalem, he named the council of Elders, the officers of the Temple with respect to their functions, and the sacerdotal caste as such. The intermediary between the royal government and the Jews was the High Priest, appointed by the king. Practically, the office was hereditary and was held for life. The High Priests, responsible primarily for the tribute, also became accustomed under Egyptian domination to farm the other taxes. In this way, the High Priest became the political head of the nation as well. About 190, Ben Sira spoke of the High Priest Simeon in terms appropriate to a prince: he was the glory of his people, in his time the Temple was fortified, he protected his people. As to the common people, they were sometimes summoned to the Temple court to hear official reports on the situation and to acclaim the official speaker. Nevertheless, as Ben Sira shows, the "assembly of Elders" and even the popular "assembly in the gate" continued to regulate social life and still had judicial and administrative functions.

While politically the situation of the "nation of the Jews" was essentially the same in 175 B.C.E. as had been that of the district *Yehûd* two centuries earlier, there was a decisive change as to the state of civilization.[51] There was a mixture of population and language and a diffusion of the foreign (Hellenic) culture unparalleled in the Persian period. To begin with, there were now many Hellenic cities in Palestine. The Jewish territory was practically in the midst of Hellenic cities: Ascalon, Akko (Ptolemais), Joppa (Jaffa), Apollonia and others on the coast; Samaria, Scythopolis and Gadara in the north; Pella, Gerasa, Philadelphia (Rabbath-Amana) beyond the river Jordan; and Marisa in the south. Here the Jews came into contact with Greek men, institutions, arts, soldiers from Aetolia or Macedonia, Greek poetasters and sculptors like the creator of the fine statue of the nude Aphrodite found at Carmel recently. They could see in Marisa, for instance, the Greek system of paved streets forming quadrangular blocks with a large open place at the main street, enlarged by colonnades, a view quite different from the maze that constituted an Oriental town. In Trans-Jordan there was a mixed settlement of Jewish and Greek soldiers under the command of a Jewish sheikh. There, in 259 B.C.E., a Greek from Cnidus in the service of this sheikh sold a Babylonian girl to a Greek traveler from Egypt. Among the guarantors and witnesses were a son of one Ananias and a Macedonian "of the cavalrymen of Tobias."

The Jewish territory itself was crowded with Greek officers, civil agents and traders, as the papyri show. Greek residents loaned money, bought and sold slaves, oil, wine, honey, figs, dates, while wheat was exported from Galilee. Greek caravans came up to Jerusalem too. On the other hand, the kings had inherited from the Persian monarchs grown lands, and there were in Judea estates belonging to royal courtiers. It happened, of course, as a papyrus tells, that a Greek usurer was driven out of a Jewish village when he tried to collect money for a debt; but, as this instance shows, even the village could not avoid the Greek commercial penetration. Another important factor was that now a foreign language, Greek, became that of business and administration. Even in the villages there must have been persons able to draft a contract in Greek, or to write a request in the style required for a Greek petition.

The influence of a new, foreign and technologically superior civilization acted, as usual, as a powerful dissolvent which destroyed the traditional discipline of life. The author of the Book of Jubilees[52] gives us insight into the moral situation of Palestinian Jewry after one and a half centuries of intensive contact with the Greeks. He fulminates against the evil generation who forgot the commandments and sabbaths. He repeatedly warns against associating with the pagans or eating with them. He lets Abraham implore his sons "not to take to themselves wives from the daughters of Canaan," nor to make idols and worship them. He even speaks of children of Israel "who will not circumcise their sons," and stresses the prohibition against appearing naked, that is, participating in Greek athletic games. It is particularly notable that he claims that the commandments were already observed by the Patriarchs and stresses again and again that ritual prescriptions are eternal ordinances. In fact, "every mouth speaking iniquity" already began to deny the perpetual force of the biblical regulations. As Esau says in the Book of Jubilees, "neither the children of men nor the beasts of the earth" have any oath valid forever: an echo of Greek philosophical criticism. Another contemporary writer, Ben Sira, speaks of the Jews who are ashamed of the Torah and its regulations, of ungodly men who have forsaken the Law of the Most High God. At the same time, probably unknown to Ben Sira, in Rome another adversary of Hellenism, Cato the Censor, applied himself to the reformation of the lax morals of Hellenized Rome where the newly coined word *pergraecari*, "act as a Greek," was used to signify the licentious way of life. But Cato surpassed the Jewish moralists in his antialien feelings. Ben Sira knows that wisdom has gained possession of every people and every nation, and he considers the physician ordained by God. Cato insists that Greek physicians came to Rome with the purpose of killing Romans by treatment, and under his influence Greek philosophers were expelled from Rome.

Nevertheless, it is rather difficult to gauge the impact of Greek civilization on Jewish thought in the third century B.C.E. Even if the Book of Kohelet (Ecclesiastes) was composed in this period, as the critics generally agree, it hardly shows any trace of Greek speculation. The outlook of the author is rather anti-intellectual: "he that increaseth knowledge, increaseth sorrow" (Eccl. 1:18). The whole philosophy of expediency which the author preaches, and even his lesson—make the best of the present day—belongs to the traditional teaching of wise men in the Orient. Significant only is his omission of traditional values. He does not attack these, but he emphatically denies their value: it is the same whether one sacrifices or not, "all things come alike to all" (Eccl. 9:2), "moment and chance" rule life (Eccl. 3:19). Ecclesiastes is

61

prepared to accept anything because he doubts the value of everything. He mentions God thirty-eight times, but he also repeats thirty times that "all is vanity." It is in opposition to such a philosophy of relativity, dear to the "sons of Belial," that the author of Jubilees stresses the heavenly origin of the traditional precepts of belief and ritual.

As it often happens, in order to uphold traditional values, their apologists themselves propose the most radical innovations. The author of the Book of Jubilees outdoes the later talmudic teaching in his severity as to the observance of ritual prescriptions. But to assert the everlasting validity of the Torah, this traditionalist places his own composition beside and even above Scripture, claims for his book a divine origin, and gives precepts which differ widely from those set forth in the Torah. The Bible says that the sun and the moon shall regulate seasons and days. In his paraphrase the author of Jubilees attacks the lunisolar calendar and strongly urges the adoption of his own system of a year of 364 days in which each holiday always falls on the same day of the week as ordained by God. Since the Jewish ecclesiastic calendar was built on the observation of the physical reappearance of the new moon, the apologist of orthodoxy simply proposes to turn upside down the whole structure of the ritual. The reason for his revolutionary idea is significant: the irregularity of the moon confuses the times. Thus, without realizing it, this traditionalist succumbs to the seduction of the Greek penchant for rationalization.

In the face of innovators, Hellenistic or pseudo-orthodox, the conservative forces, grouped around the Temple, stood fast and tried to uphold the established way of life.[50]

The literary representative of this conservative class was Jesus Ben Sira, a warm admirer of the High Priest Simeon. He realized that with him a venerable line of pious maxim writers came to an end: "I, indeed, came last of all," he says, "as one that gleaneth after the grape-gatherers." His social and religious ideas are conventional and the advice he addresses to his "son" (that is, pupil) aims at making him accept the present order. "The works of God are all good and He provides for every need in its time." Although he sharply denounces the oppressors who, by the multitude of their sacrifices, try to pacify God for sins—he that deprives the hireling of his hire sheds blood—he is convinced that poverty and wealth alike come from God. In these views, Ben Sira reproduces the traditional wisdom of the Orient. This traditional Oriental wisdom is further reflected in such general dicta as "he that runs after gold will not be guiltless." He also keeps the traditional tenets of religion, and implicitly rejects the new doctrine of the future life. He maintains that man can dominate his evil nature by strictly following the Law, he clings to the principle that the moral govern the world, that the wicked are punished, and that virtue leads to well-being while laziness and dissolution bring disaster. He strongly stresses man's own responsibility for his sins and his advice to his pupils is biblical: "with all thy strength love Him that made thee."

Historians classify, but life's strands are inextricably interwoven. The traditionalist Ben Sira is at the same time the first Jewish author to put his own name to his work and to emphasize his literary personality and individuality. He claims no prophetic inspiration, nor any apocalyptic revelation. He is bringing doctrine "for all those who seek instruction" and, like a Greek wandering philosopher of his time, proclaims: "Hear me, you great ones of the people and give ear to me, you, rulers of the congregation." He not only accepts the figure of personified wisdom (an originally Canaanite goddess), which appears in Proverbs, but puts this profane knowledge on a level with "the book of the

Covenant of the Most High, the law which Moses commanded"—a rather bold effort to reconcile the synagogue with the Greek Academy, Jerusalem with Athens. Even the literary form of his book reflects the modernism which he combats. Ben Sira is fond of utilizing passages of Scripture as texts to comment upon in putting forth his own views on the subject. This practice was probably influenced by synagogue preaching.

The process of action and reaction produced in the third century B.C.E. by the suddenly intensified contact between Judaism and Hellenism led to curious changes in the usage of the Divine Name. The proper name of the national God (YHWH) ceased to be pronounced by the Jews in the course of the fifth century except in the Temple service and in taking an oath. The latter usage is attested to by a source used by Philo,[54] and it was preserved by the Samaritans as late as the fifth century of the Common Era. As the exceptions show, the motive for the disuse of the proper name was the idea that its utterance had magical power. The general belief in the magical efficacy of the proper name is well known, but in Canaan it became dominant about the beginning of the first millennium B.C.E. Thus, the Phoenician gods are anonymous[55] while the deities of the "Proto-Phoenicians" in the fourteenth century B.C.E. had proper names, as the texts of Ugarit show. The Jews accepted the idea of the unpronounceable Divine Name, only after the Exile. Their national God was now "the God in Jerusalem" or the "God of Heaven," a name which identified Him with the supreme deity of the Persians and the Syrian peoples. Accordingly, the pronunciation *Elohim* (God), and afterward *Adonai* (my Lord), was substituted for the tetragrammaton YHWH. When the Greeks came, the abstract term, "God," perfectly corresponded to their philosophical conception of the Supreme Being, *ho Theos,* the God, or *to Theion,* the Divine. So they accepted this indefinite designation for the God of the Jews. By a kind of reversed attraction, the Greek speculative term then influenced Hebrew writers. The Book of Kohelet speaks of God only as *Elohim.* One would expect, therefore, that when speaking Greek the Jews would designate their God as *ho Theos* or *to Theion.* As a matter of fact, they said *Kyrios,* a legal term meaning the legitimate master of someone or something, a word which as a substantive was not used in Greek religious language. It is simply a literal translation of the Hebrew appellative *Adonai* (the Lord), which became in the meantime the standard pronunciation of the awe-inspiring tetragrammaton. Since *Kyrios* was not intelligible to the Greeks and the term *Theos* had a rather general meaning, the Jews speaking or writing Greek in Palestine began in the third century B.C.E. to speak of their God as *Hypsistos,* "the Most High." In the same way, in the fifth century B.C.E. the Hellenized Thracians identified their supreme deity, *Sabazios,* with Zeus. And again, the Greek term reacted upon the Hebrew style. Already in Ben Sira the designation, "Most High God," is found forty-eight times, although the corresponding Hebrew term *Elyon* is very rare in the Bible. The same circumlocution is frequently used by the very anti-Greek author of the Book of Jubilees, and the same title was chosen by the Maccabean priest-kings to designate the God of Zion in their official Hebrew utterances. The Talmud quotes the formula: "In such a year of Johanan, priest of the Most High God."

But the most important result of the Greek impact on Palestinian Judaism was the formation of a Jewish intelligentsia, different from the clergy and not dependent on the sanctuary. The new class was known as "scribes." "Scribe," if not simply penman, was the technical term for a public official who entered the civil service as a profession. Accordingly, there were in the acient Orient preparatory schools for future office-holders. From these institutions came the works of the mundane "wisdom" literature (like the biblical Proverbs), advising, as a Babylonian text says, "to fear God and the Law." But in the Hellenistic age Greek became the universal language of administration and business, and native writing and learning were rapidly becoming confined to the temples. The cuneiform documents of the Hellenistic age use the ideogram "priest" to denote the native notaries, and the latter act in Ptolemaic Egypt "in behalf" of a priest. Likewise, the native law in Ptolemaic Egypt was administered by a court of three priests. In both Egypt and Babylonia, so far as the native writing was still used, the priest was now the scribe, the judge and the sole teacher of the people, and the temples were only centers of native learning. The "Chaldeans," astrologers and astronomers who preserved the ancient science in Babylonia, were part of the clergy. At the same time as in Egypt and Mesopotamia the polytheistic Orient shrinks into a priestly dependence, there begins a cleavage between the sacerdotal and the secular interpreters of the Divine Law in Judaism. About 190 B.C.E. Ben Sira urges his hearers to honor the priest and to give him his portion according to the Law. He acknowledges the authority of the High Priest "over statutes and judgment," but it is the scribe who advises the rulers, and the assembly in the gate sits in the seat of the judge and expounds righteousness and judgment. The scribe is not a lawyer acting in behalf of a client; but like the Roman *juris periti* of the same period, a person who has such knowledge of the laws and customs as to act as authority for the judge to follow in his decisions. In both Jerusalem and Rome, the administration of justice was no longer in the hands of the priests in the third century B.C.E. Ecclesiastes mentions the "ten rulers" of the city who are not worth one Sage (Eccl. 7:19). Ben Sira mentions the jursdiction of the popular assembly in the punishment of adultery. But for the most part he speaks of the "rulers." He advises his reader: Gain instruction so that you may "serve the potentate." Ben Sira has in mind the agents of the Macedonian kings, such as Zenon, well known on account of recently discovered papyri. As servant of his Greek master, the Jewish scribe becomes a legitimate interpreter of the Divine Law. In fact, still at the time of Malachi, that is, toward the end of the fifth century B.C.E., knowledge comes from the priest's lips and the people "seek the law at his mouth; for he is the messenger of the Lord of hosts" (Mal. 2:7). It is the priest who answers the questions concerning ritual cleanliness (Hag. 2:12). The Chronicler still regards instruction in the Law as the privilege and duty of the Levites and considers the "scribes" as a class of the Levites (II Chron. 34:13). But in the royal charter given to Jerusalem in 200 B.C.E. the "scribes of the sanctuary" form a special and privileged body. The foreign rulers of the Orient needed, of course, expert advice as to the laws and customs of their subjects. Antiochus III's proclamation concerning the ritual arrangements at Jerusalem could not be drafted without the collaboration of Jewish jurists. At the same time, the lay scribe, powerful in the council of the Greek potentates, became, owing to his influence with the foreign master, an authority in the Jewish assembly. "The utterance of a prudent man," says Ben Sira, "is sought for in the congregation," and he mentions in opposition to the scribe, the craftsman, whose opinion is not asked in the council of the people. Since all Jewish law and legal customs were derived from the Torah, the scribe became the authority as to the Law of Moses. He meditated on the Law of the Most High. But still, in the time of Ben Sira the knowledge of the Torah was considered only part of the intellectual qualifications required of the scribe. He had also to find out the hidden sense of parables and to search out the wisdom of all the ancients. Daniel, who explains the secret and meaning of royal dreams at the Babylonian court, is the ideal scribe as visualized by Ben Sira. On the other hand, the scribe is not only counselor of kings and assemblies, but also wise man and teacher. "Turn to me, you ignorant," says Ben Sira, "and tarry in my school." He promises as the fruit of his teaching the acquisition by the pupil of "much silver and gold." But he gives to his pupils "wisdom," "and all wisdom cometh from the Lord." So his scribe and his school of wisdom prepare for the coming of the Pharisaic scholar in the next generation. This Pharisaic scholar regards learning as the highest of human values and teaches that the fear of the Lord is the beginning of wisdom, but is prepared to serve his Master not for the sake of reward. However, between Ben Sira and the first Pharisees, there is the persecution of Antiochus and the revolution of the Maccabees.

The process of dispersion continued and created new ramifications of third-century Jewry. We learn, for instance, that toward the end of this century two thousand Jewish families from Babylonia were settled by the Seleucid government as military colonists in Lydia and Phrygia, and that at the beginning of the same century Ptolemy I transferred Jews and Samaritans from Palestine to Egypt. The wars between Alexander's successors brought many Jewish slaves, captured in Palestine, to the Alexandrian or Syrian markets. There was also a voluntary emigration; many went to Egypt, we are told, attracted by the humanity of the Ptolemies.

The bulk of Jewry was still established between the Euphrates and the Nile. But the fate of Alexander's empire divided the Levant into two parts. While the Jews of Egypt and, until 200 B.C.E., of Palestine owed allegiance to the Ptolemies, the Jews in the East and, after 200 B.C.E., in Palestine, were subjects of the Seleucids. The Hellenistic kingdoms were based on personal loyalty to the monarch rather than on national or territorial feeling. Since the Seleucids and the Ptolemies were perpetual rivals and antagonists who fought five wars in the third century, both dynasties tried to gain the favor of the Jews. It is significant that the biblical passage (Deut. 26:5), "A wandering Aramean was my father and he went down into Egypt," is changed to "My father forsook Syria and went down into Egypt" in the Alexandrian Greek version. Likewise, the Midrash for Passover evening, established by the authorities of the Temple under the Egyptian rule, changes the same scriptural sentence, giving to it the meaning that the "Aramean," that is, Laban, the personification of Syria, sought to destroy "my father," Jacob, so that the latter came to Egypt according to the Word of God. On the other hand, after 200 B.C.E., under the Seleucid domination, another composition in the Passover service put emphasis upon the anti-Egyptian implications of the Exodus and upon Israel's Mesopotamian origins.[56] The fact that Jerusalem, the spiritual center of the Diaspora, belonged to one of the rival powers cast suspicion on the loyalty of the Jews under the domination of the other. In a paraphrase of the biblical history, the Book of Jubilees explains the enslavement of the Jews by Pharaoh

73

as follows: "because their hearts and faces are toward the land of Canaan," ruled by the king of Syria.

In the light of these texts we may understand the origins of the Alexandrine version of the Bible. According to Jewish tradition, already known and standardized about 180 B.C.E., the Greek translation of the Torah was made about 280-250 B.C.E. in Alexandria upon the suggestion of King Ptolemy II. Modern critics reject the tradition without the slightest reason, and regard the undertaking as one of the Alexandrine community, intended to convert the heathen and to enable the Greek-speaking Jews to read the Scriptures.

Regardless of the auspices under which this translation was undertaken, the mere fact that the translation was made is of primary importance. Let us add that the Greek version of the Torah was soon followed by translations of other Jewish books. Throughout three centuries and more, the Jews did not cease from rendering their books into the world's common language. Psalms of the Temple and the Psalms ascribed to Solomon, the prophets of old and the new fabricated revelations of Enoch and Moses, Job and Esther and the chronicles of the Maccabean dynasty were published in Greek. Looking back at this activity of translators, a later Rabbi explained Genesis 9:27 as meaning: "Let them speak the language of Japhet in the tent of Shem."[57]

This venture of translating was unique in antiquity. There were in Greek some popular tales or missionary tracts adapted from Egyptian; some authentic traditions were preserved in Greek books which circulated under the name of Zoroaster or Ostanes. Contemporary with the Greek version of the Torah, an Egyptian priest (Manetho) and the Chaldean Berossus, and later some Phoenician authors, issued in Greek summaries "from the sacred books" of the history of their respective peoples. These compilations were, like similar works of Jewish or Roman writers, Demetrius, Fabius Pictor and later Flavius Josephus, adaptations made to Greek taste.

However, the esoteric character of priestly lore prevented a wholesale translation of the sacred books of the East. We know exactly hymns and rites of the Babylonian temples at Uruk (the biblical Erech) as used in the Hellenistic age, since we are able to decode the cuneiform signs. But the priests who copied these texts under the rule of the Seleucids abstained from translating their psalms and instructions into Greek. No wonder: in describing some rites, the author of the ancient text added: "The Foreigner may not see it." Likewise, there is an abundant literature in Greek attributed to the Egyptian god of wisdom, Thoth, called in Greek Hermes. But these books hardly exhibit any Egyptian element, and the ignorance of their writers is such that they make "That," which is another spelling of "Thoth," refer to an independent divinity. Although the daily liturgy of Hellenized gods, such as Isis, was celebrated in Greek, the authentic sacred books of Egypt, carried by the priests in sacral processions, remained inaccessible to the Hellenes. An immense body of literature in Greek was ascribed to Zoroaster, but none of his votaries took the trouble to translate his authentic Hymns, and the Persian god Mithra always remained "unable to speak Greek."

In this way, while the Oriental religions remained unknown to a Western devotee, they lost ground in their native countries as well when the hieroglyphs and the cuneiforms began to be forgotten. In the second century B.C.E. the knowledge of sacred letters was already limited at Uruk in Babylonia to a small group of clerics. By translating liberally its literature, sacred and profane, new and old, into the world language, Judaism preserved its vitality. Moses and his law, or the revelations of Jewish seers, entered and filled in the mental world of the proselytes as if the latter had been born in Abraham's posterity. The Jews became "people of the Book" when this Book was rendered into Greek.

To return to the Greek version of the Torah, it was done with due regard for the Greek reader. The Rabbinic tradition recalls the fact that the translators at times changed their text out of deference to pagan sensitivity.

A classic instance is Lev. 11:6, where the Greek version renders the word "hare" among the unclean animals by "rough foot," because the Greek word for hare *(Lagos)* was the epithet for the ancestor of the Ptolemaic Dynasty. Even more important is the religious terminology of the translation. Although the ineffable Name was transliterated in the Greek Bible it was pronounced as *Kyrios*, the Lord. Likewise, the version omits other appellations of the God of Israel, such as *Adonai, Shaddai, Sabaot*, which continued to be used in Palestine. In their place, the version employs expressions such as "the God," "the Almighty," etc. In this way the particular God of Abraham, Isaac and Jacob becomes in Greek the Supreme Being of mankind. This representation of the original meaning corresponds to the religious trend of the Greek world. In the Greek Diaspora the local deities, let us say of Thebes or Crete, gave place to the universal Olympians, and the latter, losing their individuality, became simply different forms of the same universal deity of salvation and benefaction.

Consider another example. The term, "Torah," should be rendered in Greek by words expressing some kind of authority. But its regular rendering in the version is *Nomos*, "the Law," or better, "the constitution." Thus, the Pentateuch in Greek appeared as the legal corpus of Jewry. But while the translators tried to present Judaism as universalistic, they were no less intent on emphasizing the difference between the true religion and heathenism. For instance, they purposely used different Greek terms when speaking of the Temple or the Altar or the service of the true God and, on the other hand, when mentioning idolatry. In a hymn of praise, written in 261 B.C.E., a Greek contemporary of the translators glorified the Egyptian deity who had cured him.[58] The technical terms of praise he uses, such as *arete, dynamis, kratos* do not occur, with regard to the Lord, in the Greek Pentateuch. With the same purpose of separating the Supreme Being from the anthropomorphic idols of the Greeks, the version avoids expressions attributing human forms and passions to the Lord.

For instance, Ex. 24:10 tells that the Elders coming up toward Sinai with Moses "saw the God of Israel." The Greek version reads: they saw the place "where the God of Israel had stood." But neither the Greek version of the Bible nor the works of Berossus and Manetho, written for the Greek public, attained their object. The Greeks preferred their own quite fantastic versions of Oriental history. They repeated, for instance, despite Berossus' protest, that Babylon was founded by the dissolute Queen Semiramis, and said that Judah, the ancestor of the Jews, was a son of the same legendary queen. Neither Berossus nor Manetho is quoted by Greek historians, but both were read and used as sources of astrological and magical knowledge. Likewise, the Septuagint is quoted a few times by philosophers. Later pagan speculation might, like the author of *Poimandres*, employ the biblical history of creation to express a new religious feeling. But Greek scholarship intentionally ignored the Bible as well as Berossus or Manetho because the Greeks regarded, quite naturally, their own tradition of the mythical past as trustworthy and consequently rejected as unreliable myths the contradictory Oriental accounts.

Relations between the Jews and the pagans in the Dispersion continued to be friendly or indifferent. Philosophers considered the strict observance of the Sabbath as superstition. A writer could reproduce the malicious anecdote, invented by the Idumeans, about the foolishness of the people of Jerusalem. But there is no anti-Jewish passage in Greek literature before the Maccabean struggle nor any recorded anti-Jewish action. The details of daily life of the Jews in the Diaspora before the Maccabean age are almost unknown, except for Egypt. Here we find Jews transacting business with other colonists. They were legally regarded as "Hellenes," in opposition to the native "Egyptians." There is, for instance, a judgment of a Ptolemaic court of 226 B.C.E. concerning an alleged assault. Both parties were Jews, but the legal guardian of the defendant, a Jewess, was an Athenian, the witnesses of the summons were a Thracian and a Persian, and the case was decided according to Greek law. The juridical situation of the Jews in Ptolemaic Egypt, and in the Diaspora generally, is sufficiently clear. The difficulty begins when we try to appreciate the cultural relations between Jews and pagans. The number "6" was called "Eve of Sabbath" in the slang of gamblers in Alexandria.[59] What did the Greeks know of the Jewish religion? Around 200 B.C.E. a Jewish poetaster wrote a tragedy describing the Exodus. The author

(Ezekiel) follows Hellenistic dramatic techniques and imitates Euripides. But was his composition written for heathen readers or was it intended to take the place in Jewish education of Greek plays based on mythology? The most impressive witness and the most important feature of Judaism coming into contact with Hellenism was the conversion of Greeks. There were, of course, always "strangers who joined themselves unto the Lord" (Jub. 55:10), but it was only in the Hellenistic age that proselytism became widespread. To understand the phenomenon, let us note at the outset that new adherents unto the Lord were all, or almost all, Greeks or Hellenized natives of Greek cities. The people of the countryside continued to speak their native languages and stubbornly worshiped their traditional gods. An Anatolian or Egyptian peasant did not care much for any deity in Greek garb, whether from Olympus or from Zion. The Greek translation of the Pentateuch represented the Most High God of the Dispersion as speaking Greek. The Alexandrine version of the Torah was made before 250 B.C.E. No part of the Bible, however, was translated by the Jews into any tongue other than Greek—not even Latin, although some Latin formulae were used by Latin-speaking Jews in Africa and Italy in the second and third centuries C.E.

All translations of the Bible, except those into Greek, were the results of Christian missionary activity. The Ethiopian eunuch, returning from a pilgrimage to Jerusalem, was reading Isaiah (Acts 8:28) in Greek when met by the Apostle Philip on the road. Probably no Jew in Egypt ever tried to reach the natives who spoke only dialects of the Egyptian tongue. He was "Hellene" and as such he discriminated against the people who did not know Greek. Nothing seemed to him more unfair than the idea of degrading himself to the condition of the natives. On the other hand, the people of the cities were in a propitious mood to receive foreign missionaries. The new cities of the Near East were new homes for settlers whether they came from Athens or from Caria. Of course, everybody took with him to his new home his ancestral idols and did not neglect the age-old shrines of the new country's deities. But gods and men alike were upset on a new soil. There was room for unknown deities who might stir new hopes and quiet fears; and there was the fascinating appeal of the divine forces of the mysterious East, of gods who were old before the birth of Zeus.[60] Accordingly, many Oriental cults started missionary efforts among the "Hellenes." An Egyptian priest brought the worship of Serapis to Delos, the sacred island of the

Greeks, at about the beginning of the third century
B.C.E. A shrine was erected to the Syrian Atargatis
in an Egyptian village by a Macedonian soldier in
222 B.C.E. Before the end of the third century B.C.E.
the mysteries of the Persian Mithra spread among
the Greeks in Egypt. Jewish propaganda followed
the same road and the same pattern. The same
term *proselytos (advena)*,[61] that is "one who has
arrived at or to," was used for both the converts
to the Lord and the converts to the Egyptian Isis.
Unfortunately, we do not have dated evidence of
Jewish proselytism before the Maccabean period.
But when we are told that in 139 B.C.E. Jews were
expelled from Rome for attempting "to infect"
Roman morals with their cult, we may postulate
that proselytism in the Near East must have started
before the beginning of the second century B.C.E.
It seems that in early Hellenism the people who
completely accepted Judaism by circumcision and
baptism, and refused to take part any longer in
pagan ceremonies, were rather rare. But there were
numerous Hellenes who revered the Most High
without observing all the prescriptions of the
Torah. Some early Hellenistic texts throw light on
the state of mind of such "God-fearers."[62] About 180
B.C.E. a minister of Seleucus IV of Syria attempted
to extort money from the Temple treasury, but

83

failed ignominiously. His defeat, immortalized by Raphael's *Storia di Eliodoro*, was, of course, explained in Jerusalem as a miracle. The story was told of Heliodorus who, scourged by angels, had been ordered to "declare unto all men the mighty power of God." He then testified to all men the works of the Great God, whom he had seen with his eyes. Heliodorus did not become a Jew but the stripes received at the hands of the angels convinced him that the Lord of Zion is above all gods (II Macc. 2:4). In the same way, according to Jewish legend, Alexander the Great prostrated himself before the High Priest, and Nebuchadnezzar had to recognize that the Most High God does according to His will, "in the host of heaven and among the inhabitants of the earth" (Dan. 4:32).

Since pagan cults were polytheistic, their propaganda tried to persuade men only of the relative superiority of a particular deity. The Jewish mission adopted the same pattern. For example, there is a Jewish tale of Bel and Daniel. Deceived by a trick of Bel's priests, the Persian king exclaims, "Great art thou, Bel, and there is not with him deceit." But Daniel explodes the pretended miracle, and the king recognizes that great is the Lord, God of Daniel, and there is none other beside Him. The Book of Jonah describes a Jewish missionary who calls for repentance and is sent to foreign lands, where the name of the Lord is already known and revered. The sailors on Jonah's ship are heathen, praying, every man, to his own idol, but they all fear the Lord exceedingly. These sailors, or Heliodorus of the Jewish tale, resemble the adherents of syncretistic cults who worshiped the Lord as the Supreme Master of the Universe, but placed under Him, or beside Him, other divine forces. Such were, for example, some religious societies in Asia Minor which fused the Phrygian *Sabazios* with *Sabaot,* observed the Sabbath, but refused to accept the exclusive attitude of Judaism toward pagan worship. The existence of such "God-fearers" extended the influence of Judaism, of course, and the sons of semiproselytes often became full converts. But the recognition of such followers of Judaism sapped the foundations of the latter. A Jewish latitudinarian, such as a certain Artapanus, could endeavor to identify Moses with Thot-Hermes, a central figure in Hellenistic syncretism, and ascribe to the apostle of monotheism the establishment of the Egyptian cult of animals.

On the other hand, let us again open the Book of Jonah. The people of Nineveh who were and who remained pagans did not perish because they fasted and, covered with sackcloth, cried mightily unto God. Such is the lesson of this book: God is abundant in mercy and will have pity on the great city "wherein are more than sixscore thousand persons that cannot discern between their right hand and their left hand, and also much cattle." The design of the book is not to teach the universality of Divine grace, as the critics say today. This point is already presumed by the author. But as the Rabbis explained and the Church Father, Chrysostom, saw, the question of Jonah is whether contrition per se, even that of unbelievers, is sufficient to turn away God's anger. The Jewish author of the bibilical book affirms it. The universal church, as well as the mosque, answers in the negative—*extra ecclesiam nulla salus*. This answer as well as Jonah's misgivings about God's compassion are easy to understand. If the repentance of the unbeliever avails him, if he may share the favor of Heaven without assuming the yoke of the Law, why the necessity to enter the fold? Why should a Jew by birth observe the numberless minute ritual precepts which involve social disapproval and, for instance, bar him from the royal table? The generous universalism of the Book of Jonah was more dangerous to institutional Judaism than the indifference of Ecclesiastes. The confusion of the syncretists helped to inspire the reform of the Jewish religion about 175 B.C.E. under the auspices of Antiochus Epiphanes.

NOTES

1. *Herod*, III, 19.
2. See the present writer's paper "An Edict of Cyrus," in *Journ. of Bibl. Lit.*, LXV, 1944.
3. Berosus ap. Josephus, *Contra Apionem*, I, 150.
4. Maurice Holleaux, *Etudes d'épigraphie et d'histoire grecques*, (Paris, 1938), I, i.
5. On Sephararvain cf. William Foxwell Albright, *Archaeology and the Religion of Israel* (Baltimore, 1942), p. 163.
6. On chronology cf. Albright, *op. cit.*, p. 168.
7. See A. Dupont-Sommer, *Revue de l'histoire des religions*, CXXX (Paris, 1945, 17-28) and *Comptes-Rendus de l'Académie des Inscriptions* (1947), *pp.* 175-191.
8. Sidney Smith, *Babylonian Historical Texts* (London, 1924), p. 145.
9. Albright, "Light on the Jewish State in Persian Times," in *Bull. Amer. Sch. Or. Res.*, No. 53, p. 20.
10. M. Rostovtzeff, *Social and Economic History of the Hellenistic World*. (Oxford, 1941) III, 1324.
11. On the so-called "Naucratis" inscription see the literature quoted by G. Posener in *Annales du Service des Antiques de l'Egypte* (Paris, 1934), p. 141.
12. See E. Bikerman, "Héliodore au Temple de Jérusalem," in *Annuaire de l'Institut de Philologie et d'Histoire Orientales* (Université de Bruxelles), 1939-1942, VII, 14.
13. Hecataeus ap. Jos *C. Ap.* I. 188.

[14] For archaeological evidence cf. Rostovtzeff, *op. cit.,* p. 1325. see also McCown, *Tell En-Nashbeh,* I (Berkeley, 1947).

[15] Clearchus ap. Jos. *C. Ap.* I, 176, Cf. Hans Lewy, "Aristotle and the Jewish Sage According to Clearchus of Soli," in *Harv. Theo. Rev.,* XXXI, No. 3, p. 205.

[16] A. Reifenberg, *Ancient Jewish Coins* (Jerusalem, 1947).

[17] Reifenberg, *op. cit.* #Ia. A Hebrew shekel (3.88gr.) in silver, obv.: male head bearded; Rv.: Female head; Inscr. (in Hebrew): "one half."

[18] Reifenberg, *op. cit.,* Plate I, #3.

[19] Louis Finkelstein, *The Pharisees* (Philadelphia, 1938), II, p. 566.

[20] C. C. Torrey, *The Second Isaiah* (New York, 1928), p. 126, has already vigorously protested against this misconception. cf. Finkelstein, *op. cit.,* p. 461.

[21] It is a pity that N. D. Fustel de Coulanges's *La Cité Antique,* published in 1864, is almost unknown outside of France.

[22] Eur., *Electra,* 795.

[23] Eur., *Ion,* 588.

[24] Cf. A. D. Nock, *Conversion* (London, 1933), p. 20.

[25] Eur., *Heracl.,* 348.

[26] A. T. Olmstead, *History of Assyria* (New York, 1923), p. 580.

[27] Cf. Albright, *From the Stone Age to Christianity* (Baltimore, 1929), pp. 242 and 245.

[28] G. Glotz, *The Greek City and its Institutions* (New York, 1929), p. 258.

[29] C. N. Cochrane, *Christianity and Classical Culture* (Oxford, 1944), p. 462.

[30] Dion. Halic., *De. Thuc.* 5. I quote the translation of the passage in Lionel Pearson, *Early Ionian Historians* (Oxford, 1939), p. 3.

[31] Adolf Erman, *The Literature of the Ancient Egyptians* (London, 1927), pp. 58 and 95.

[32] Cf., too, an inscription of Shalmaneser III in D. D. Lucken-bill, *Ancient Records of Assyria and Babylonia* (Chicago, 1926-1927), II. The narrative begins in the first person (#623) and continues in the third person (#624).

[33] R. W. Rogers, *Cuneiform Parallels to the Old Testament* (New York, 1912), p. 380.

[34] Such fictitious documents are already included in the Egyptian cycle of stories of Petubastis, a kind of historical novel which is presented as a work of historiography. See G. Maspero, *Popular Stories of Ancient Egypt,* (New York, 1915), pp. 242 and 256.

[35] See Rostovtzeff, *op. cit.,* III, 1326.

[36] *Herod,* II, 30 and 154.

[37] Albright, "King Joachim in Exile," in *Biblical Archaeologist,* V, No. 4, p. 51.

[38] W. Eilers, in *Zeitschr. Deutsch. Morgenlaend. Ges.,* 1940, p. 225.

[39] See S. Daiches, *The Jews of Babylonia,* (London, 1910).

[40] A. E. Cowley *Aramaic Papyri of the Fifth Century* (Oxford, 1923). Some 125 ostraca will be published by A. Dupont-Sommer. See his papers quoted above in n. 7.

[41] E. Dhorme in *Revue d'Assyriologie,* 1928.

[42] F. L. Griffith, *Catalogue of the Demotic Papyri in the John Rylands Library* (Manchester, 1909), p. 60.

[43] See Bickerman, "Un Document retalif à la persécution d'Antiochus IV Epiphane," in *Revue de l'Histoire des Religions,* CXV, p. 188.

[44] Lewy, "Hekataios von Abdera," in *Zeitschr. Neutest. Wissen.,* XXXI, p. 117.

[45] W. Jaeger, "Greeks and Jews: The First Greek Records of Jewish Religion and Civilization," in *Journal of Religion,* XVIII, p. 38.

[46] Lewy, *op. cit.,* n. 15.

[47] We do not know whether oil was also distributed to the people who did not frequent the "gymnasia." Cf. Jeanne et Louis Robert, *Inscriptions grecques de Lydie,* p. 129.

[48] F. Pfister, "Eine juedische Gruendungsgeschichte Alexandrias," in *Sitz. Heidelberger Akad. Wissen.*, XI, July, 1914.

[49] See Bikerman, *Institutions des Séleucides* (Paris, 1938), p. 165.

[50] Polybius, XVI, 39, 5.

[51] Rostovtzeff, *op. cit.*, Index s.v. Palestine.

[52] On the Book of Jubilees: Finkelstein, "Pre-Maccabean Documents in the Passover Haggadah," in *Harv. Theo. Rev.*, XXXVI, p. 19.

[53] On the phantom of the so-called "Great Synagogue," which is often evoked by modern writers on this period, see my note xxxi in *Revue Biblique*, 1948.

[54] W. L. Knox, *Some Hellenistic Elements in Primitive Christianity* (London, 1944), p. 48.

[55] See Bickerman, "Anonymous Gods," in *Journ. of the Warburg Inst.*, I, p. 58.

[56] Finkelstein, "The Oldest Midrash: Pre-Rabbinic Ideals and Teachings in the Passover Haggadah," in *Harv. Theo. Rev.*, XXXI, p. 291 and XXXVI, p. 19.

[57] S. Lieberman, *Greek in Jewish Palestine*, (Philadelphia, 1942).

[58] See Bataille's paper quoted in n. 67.

[59] P. Perdrizet, in *Bull. de l'Inst. Français d'Archéol. Orient.*, XXX, 5.

[60] See the classic book of Franz Cumont, *Les religions orientales dans le paganisme romain* (4th ed., Paris, 1929).

[61] R. Reitzenstein, *Die hellenistischen Mysterienreligionen* (3rd ed., Leipzig, 1927), p. 193.

[62] See paper quoted in n. 12.

PART II

THE MACCABEES

TO T. B.

DEPORTED BY THE GERMANS

PS. 35 : 17

THE PERSECUTIONS

OF ANTIOCHUS EPIPHANES

———

At the end of the year 167 B.C.E., approximately in December, by order of Antiochus IV Epiphanes, King of Syria and so ruler of the Jews, the Temple on Zion was desecrated and given over to the uses of idolatry. At the same time the law of Moses was rescinded by a decree of the King. Observance of the commandments of the Torah, such as circumcision and the sanctification of Sabbath and New Moon, was made a capital offense. In addition, the Jews were required to worship the gods of the Gentiles. Altars were erected to these gods in every locality, and the populace was commanded to offer sacrifice to the new deities. It was the pig, precisely the animal regarded by the Jews as unclean, that was the most acceptable offering to these gods. Pigs were offered even upon the altar of the Sanctuary at Jerusalem, upon which each day, in early morning and at the approach of evening, offerings had been made to the

God of Israel. The "abomination of desolation" hovered over the Sanctuary and the wrath of God over the people. Never before and never thereafter was the spiritual existence of Israel so imperiled. Was this not the last trial, that Day of the Lord so often proclaimed and threatened by the prophets?

A book has come down to us from this period of persecution, the biblical Book of Daniel. In the midst of these afflictions a seer perceived the significance of the ancient prophecies concerning the world empires, their wars, and the tribulations of the holy people. To him, these prophecies seemed to speak of his own time, and thus he interpreted them for his contemporaries, suiting them to the events during the persecutions of Epiphanes. He felt that the end of time was approaching, and he could see no salvation for the people other than through the direct intervention of God. He knew well enough that the Romans had just driven Epiphanes from Egypt, and that the King was then waging a campaign in the East; yet he refused to think of the possibility, frequently suggested by the prophets, that another earthly power might, in fulfilment of the divine plan, crush the persecutor to earth. Rather would Epiphanes yet conquer Egypt, he foretold: ". . . and there shall be a time of trouble, such as never was since there was a nation even to that same time"—until "there came with the clouds of heaven one like unto a son of man" to rule over the world forever. The reader of this book knew that supplication and fast—but never a human act—might alter the course of events and shorten the period of tribulation.

Daniel's resignation was no accident. Judaism's cause seemed desperate precisely because the Jews showed no zeal in its defense. Two centuries later, when the Roman governor Pontius Pilate had his standards bearing the image of the emperor set up in the Temple area, the people went to his headquarters at Caesarea and for five days and five nights besought him to remove the human likenesses from the Holy City. And when Pilate's soldiers surrounded the crowd with swords drawn, the Jews bared their necks; they preferred death to acquiescence—and Pilate yielded.

But in 166 Jerusalem was filled with monuments of the pagan cult, and the princes of Jerusalem together with the men of Judea obediently heeded the will of the earthly ruler. Altars were built before the doors of the houses and sacrifices were offered upon them, to make a public display of zeal for the new paganism. Only a few proved unyielding and openly transgressed the commandment of the King for the sake of the commandment of the living God. They were seized, scourged, martyred, and slain.

More numerous were those who sought to evade the order of the King. Without standing forth openly as Jews, they still avoided any participation in the idolatrous rites. In order to lay hold of these, officers of the King journeyed from city to city, coercing the people into open apostasy. They would cause an altar to be erected in the market place, summon the populace, and require them to worship the gods and taste the flesh of the offerings. Many refused, and suffered martyrdom. "They shall stumble by the sword and by flame," says Daniel of them, "by captivity and by spoil, many days."

In the course of the winter of 166 the agents of apostasy made their appearance in the town of Modin, situated upon a hill near Lydda, on the road from Jerusalem to Jaffa. When the first Jew of Modin stepped up to the pagan altar to sacrifice according to the King's will, Mattathias, a priest whose family resided in Modin, sprang out from the circle of bystanders, struck the man down so that his body was stretched out upon the altar, slew the agent of the government, and then pulled down the altar.

In the age of the religious wars, in the sixteenth and seventeenth centuries, the legitimacy of Mat-

96

tathias' conduct was vigorously debated. His hallowed precedent was held to justify subjects who oppose the authorities in questions of faith. This conception of his deed, which is not without significance even today, would have seemed strange and perhaps dangerous to Mattathias himself. In the speech which his Jewish historian puts into his mouth Mattathias does not dispute the right of the ruler to alter the laws of peoples subject to him; he does oppose an order of the King which is at variance with the revealed commandment of God. The struggle is not one of an individual conscience for freedom of belief; it is rather a conflict between earthly power and the law of the state of God. Mattathias championed the Torah as once Phinehas had done, when he slew Zimri, who had dared worship the Baal of the Midianites (Num. 25). But looked at through the eyes of worldly power, Mattathias' deed was an act of political terrorism. Mattathias and his five sons, John (Yohanan), Simon, Judah, Eleazar, and Jonathan, fled from its punishment into the mountains of Judea.

In those days many in Israel sought out the wilderness. In order not to desecrate the holy covenant they went into the desert with "their sons, and their wives, and their cattle." Such passive resistance by flight was common in antiquity. If an Egyptian peasant was oppressed by taxes, a debtor harried by his creditor, or later a Christian persecuted for his faith, they took this means of eluding the reach of the state, whose organization was not yet so perfected as to lay hold of them. They forsook house and land and lived as wretched vagabonds, as is said of the Maccabees, "after the manner of wild beasts in the mountains." But the state suffered a falling off in revenues as a result, and yielded more and more in the course of time, until finally an amnesty was proclaimed. In the meanwhile, however, agents of the government sought to lay hands upon the fugitives. In 166 B.C.E. a search was instituted in Judea for those who had disregarded the King's command and had hidden themselves away in the wilderness. In this case the task of the police was rendered easy by a Jewish practice which seemed to the pagans the height of superstitious unreason. The Jews, lest they desecrate the day of rest, offered an attacker no resistance on the Sabbath. Thus in 312 B.C.E. Ptolemy of Egypt had been able to take possession of Jerusalem without a blow. Now, too, the fugitives made no attempt to defend themselves on the day of rest; they neither threw stones at the enemy nor walled up the caves in which they had sought safety, but preferred to die in order conscientiously to fulfil the law of God for which they had forsaken their homes.

Mattathias realized the situation: "If we all do as our brethren have done, and do not fight against the Gentiles for our lives and our ordinances, they will soon destroy us from off the earth." Mattathias and his people therefore resolved, not indeed to attack, but at least to defend themselves on the Sabbath day. This rule continued in force until the great uprising against the Romans (66-70 C.E.).

To moderns this interpretation of the fourth commandment seems the "natural" one. But it was far from being so regarded in the days of the Maccabees, as appears most clearly from the fact that the Second Book of Maccabees, which was written in the Diaspora, not only passes over the new resolution in silence but gives especial prominence to the observance of the day of rest by the Jews. It is only in the second century of the Common Era that the rabbis put forward the general principle: "The Sabbath is given to man, not man to the Sabbath."

Even more significant is the fact that Mattathias ventured to interpret the law upon his own authority. In his day this privilege was vested in the High Priest and his council, who governed Jerusalem and Judea. It was the High Priest to whom God had given "authority over statute and judgment, that he might teach His people statutes, and judgments unto the children of Israel." When Mattathias, a man previously unknown, one priest among ten thousand, resolved to interpret the traditional law, to impose his interpretation upon the people, and thus to infringe upon the prerogatives of the High Priest, he raised himself, perhaps without intending to do so, to the position of an opposition government. Hence his resolve constituted a turning point in Jewish history. His measure immediately gave him the authority of a leader. The "community of the pious," a fraternity zealous for the law of God, joined him, and his following was filled with those who fled the evil. Those who had abandoned their homes in order not to depart from the law "either to the right hand or to the left" were united by that very measure which infringed the Torah for the Torah's sake.

Strengthened by these additions, Mattathias determined upon another deed which was pregnant with consequences. Hitherto, like the other fugitives, he had evaded the royal decrees in order to seek a refuge in the desert where he might fulfil the commandments. But now the Maccabees determined to replace passive resistance by active struggle. They made a stealthy and roundabout entrance into the villages and summoned together those eager to fight; with the force thus formed they moved from place to place, destroying the idolatrous altars where they found them, compelling the observance of the Torah by force (for example, they circumcised newborn infants, as many as they found), and smiting apostate violators of the law. Thus, as their historian relates, they liberated the Torah from the hand of the heathen.

But, as is clear from this account, the wrath of the Maccabees was poured over the Jews and not the heathen. The company of the Maccabees was an active minority—Daniel calls them "a little help"—that sought to restore its law to the people. This law was in no sense an innovation, but the revelation of Moses. How came it about that this stiff-necked people backslid from the covenant of their fathers and suffered themselves to be seduced into worship of the pagan deities? Why did the struggle of the Maccabees turn into a civil war within the Jewish people? Why did it not rather become a single-hearted defense of the people against the persecutions of the Syrian king from without?

Until the time of Alexander the Great each Oriental people constituted a disparate unit, clearly differentiated from the others. Even in such a situation cultures inevitably influenced one another: the Book of Proverbs in the Bible, for example, contains many thoughts and aphorisms borrowed from the Egyptian Wisdom Book of Amenemope. Under the domination of the Persians especially, which lasted for two centuries, a great common store of beliefs and ideas developed among the various peoples. But there was no common supranational civilization; a Jew remained a Jew, as an Egyptian remained an Egyptian.

With the Greek conquest of the East (330 B.C.E.), however, the situation changed. From its beginnings Greek culture was supranational, because the Greeks never constituted a unified state. In the East, Greek colonists lost their tribal peculiarities so quickly that the innumerable Greek papyri of the period, discovered in Egypt, show no variations of dialect. The new states in the East were the creation of the Greek race of Macedonia, as Alexander himself was a Macedonian. But their culture was Panhellenic, and was the same on the Nile as on the Euphrates. The Oriental civilizations, on the other hand, were always based upon concepts of folk and religion. A man was born an Egyptian or a Jew, or became such when he forsook his own gods and served new gods. "Thy people shall be my people, and thy God my God," says the Moabitess Ruth to her Israelite mother-in-law when she resolves to follow her.

But Greek culture, like modern European culture, was based upon education. A man became a "Hellene" without at the same time forsaking his gods and his people, but merely by adopting Hellenic culture. Clearchus, a disciple of Aristotle, represents his master as conducting a conversation with a pious Jew and as calling this Jew "a Greek man not only in language but also in spirit." A century later the great geographer Eratosthenes declared that men are not to be distinguished as Greek or barbarian, but rather according to their virtues or their vices.

During the three centuries which we call Hellenistic—that is, the period between Alexander the Great and Emperor Augustus (330 to 30 B.C.E.)—the notion of the "Hellene," like the modern notion of the "European," grew into a concept independent of descent. In Hellenistic Egypt the whole population was officially divided into two classes: the natives, called the "Egyptians," and the immigrants, called the "Hellenes," regardless of their origin. In point of fact, the immigrants were Hellenized with singular rapidity. As early as the third century B.C.E. synagogues in Egypt were dedicated in honor of Greek

103

kings, and the Scriptures were translated into Greek. What could be more Hellenic and more alien to the Orientals than physical culture? But about 220 B.C.E. we find in a Samaritan settlement in Egypt a gymnasium endowed by a Cilician, whose heir was a Macedonian.

In its tendency and in its claim, therefore, Hellenistic culture was universal. To it belonged the mighty of the world and the world's dominion. It was vested with the superiority that the judgment of war constantly reaffirmed. It was open to all. Whether or not to accept this culture was therefore a question of life and death for every people. The nations of the ancient world were confronted by the same problem that confronts the Oriental peoples in the modern world from Tokyo to Cairo, whether to adopt the supranational and therefore superior European culture, or else accept an inferior status, become fellaheen. In antiquity the problem was actually solved by only two peoples, the Romans and the Jews. Other peoples shut themselves off from Hellenism, and its effects upon them were therefore only negative: the native cultures were disintegrated and enfeebled. They lost their upper class, whose connection with the people had been ruptured by the process of Hellenization. The Egyptians, for example, deprived of their upper class, their intellectual elite, for centuries lagged behind the inexorable march of history, and so suffered the fate of enslavement to foreign conquerors. "And there shall be no more a prince out of the land of Egypt."

For Judaism, then, the question of its historical existence or disappearance depended upon its ability to accommodate itself to Western culture. But in the days of the Maccabees, as in the period of Moses Mendelssohn, the law interposed a wall between Jews and non-Jews. Nothing brings people closer together than a common table. But his dietary laws forbade the Jew to taste the food of his non-Jewish neighbor. There is no closer tie than the bond of matrimony. But the Jews told with approval the story of a father who abandoned his own daughter in order to free his brother from a passing attachment to a pagan dancing girl. To a man of the Hellenistic age this "separation from the nations" could be regarded as nothing else than the expression of a Jewish "hatred of mankind." Favorably disposed critics have endeavored to explain the withdrawal of the Jews from history as the consequence of the "bad experience of their expulsion from Egypt," and to exculpate it on such grounds; but no one outside Jewry itself has ever recognized positive merit in the separation. When

105

the Jews declined to associate with pagan slave women, such an attitude seemed an invidious distinction even to a friend of the Jews, who posed the question: "Are they not human beings like yourself?"

To "advanced" Jews, therefore, it seemed imperative to let these bars fall. "In those days," we read in I Maccabees, "came there forth out of Israel lawless men, and persuaded many, saying, 'Let us go and make a covenant with the nations that are round about us; for since we separated ourselves from them many evils have come upon us.' And the saying appeared good in their eyes." "In those days" denotes the reign of the Syrian King Antiochus IV, surnamed Epiphanes (176-163 B.C.E.). The new King entrusted the position of High Priest at the Temple in Jerusalem—and hence the rule over Judea—to men of that same "advanced" party, first to a man who called himself by the Greek name of Jason (about 175-172 B.C.E.), then to Menelaus (172-162 B.C.E.). These Jewish "Hellenists" promptly received royal approval for establishing a Greek community in Jerusalem, and with it permission to erect a gymnasium. In 169, then, a regular Greek city, surrounded by walls and fortified by towers, was founded upon one of the hills of Jerusalem, opposite the Temple Mount. The

106

name of this city is unknown; in our tradition it is re-ferred to simply as Acra, that is to say, the Citadel. Henceforward the Sanctuary was dependent upon this Greek city. This was only natural. The Hellen-istic culture, understandably enough, had first af-fected the upper classes, the Jerusalemites and the priesthood. When the signal went up for the exer-cises upon the athletic field to begin, it was the priests who hastened to the contests and surrendered their priestly linens for the nakedness of Greek sports. Greek marks of distinction were prized above old-fashioned, native honors. People strove to ap-pear wholly Greek—externally, by removing the marks of circumcision through a painful operation; inwardly, by participating in the games in honor of the foreign gods, and even by contributing money for sacrifices to these gods.

But the leaders of the party understood perfectly well that all this must remain merely a diversion of the upper classes as long as the Sanctuary remained inviolate and as long as the law enjoining "misan-thropic" separation continued in force. Like the Emancipation of the nineteenth century, that of the second century B.C.E. must have necessarily led to religious "reform." But nineteenth-century Emanci-pation could in the end escape this necessity, for

Occidental civilization as a whole had in the interval become secularized.

All of ancient life was carried on within the framework of cult acts whose execution did not entail complete belief. No gymnasium could be without the images of such patron gods of athletics as Heracles and without honorific statues of the kings. Every public act was invariably accompanied by sacrifice and invariably involved prayer. To accept Western culture fully, therefore, there appeared no other alternatives than either to renounce the ancestral religion, to which any participation in the cult of the gods was an abomination, or to transform the ancient law. Many Jews of antiquity chose the first course. Among them, for example, was Tiberius Julius Alexander, nephew of the Jewish philosopher, Philo, of Alexandria. Tiberius pursued a military and administrative career that raised him to the highest stations. Among other things, he was chief of staff to Titus at the conquest of Jerusalem in 70 C.E.

Jason and Menelaus, in the reign of Epiphanes, wished to follow the other course; they desired to accommodate traditional Judaism to the times. Their intention was to preserve those characteristics of the Jewish religion which suited Greek taste—the imageless God, for example—but to remove everything which smacked of separation, of the "ghetto": Sabbath observance, beards, circumcision, and that namelessness of God which was otherwise to be met with only among the most primitive peoples.

Henceforth the Lord on Zion must bear a name which could be communicated to Greek friends who might inquire what manner of God it was that the people of Jerusalem worshipped. In Greek that name was Zeus Olympius. For some time the Jews had been in the habit of calling their God "Lord of Heaven," or even simply "Heaven," as is the regular practice in the First Book of Maccabees. But for the Greeks the Lord of Heaven was Zeus Olympius. In Aramaic the expression was probably *Baal Shemin,* under which title all the peoples of Syria worshipped the ruler of heaven. In this manner the "God of the Jews" was now accepted into the general pantheon. Now He was no longer worshipped in the dim light of the Holy of Holies, but under the open sky, in an enclosure, as was the practice in the most highly revered sanctuaries of Syria and in keeping with the Greek ideal. Even after its transformation, the cult naturally remained aniconic—educated Greeks had long ridiculed the notion that the gods had a human form. But the presence of the Almighty was now symbolized by a "sacred stone" upon the sacrificial altar in the middle of the forecourt of the Temple. All the requirements of the law concerning the sacrificial ritual were rescinded. The pig was now approved as a sacrificial animal: prohibition of its use for sacrifice or food had seemed the most striking mark of Jewish separatism.

After December of 167 B.C.E. sacrifices on Zion were carried out according to the new ritual. Offerings were made to the same God and on the same spot as formerly, but the manner was new and in direct opposition to the old. Moreover, the God of Abraham, Isaac, and Jacob was no longer sole ruler in Jerusalem. Adaptation to the religious customs of the Greeks was impossible without the surrender of monotheism. And so the festivals of Dionysus were celebrated in Jerusalem, and perhaps Athene, too, figured among the new divinities; certainly the deified kings of the ruling dynasty were included.

At the same time the High Priest Menelaus procured a decree from the King prohibiting the Mosaic law and ordering the introduction of pagan customs. Such a measure was in complete accord with the thought of the Greek social reformers, who, since Plato, had always regarded the lawgiver as the creator of social life. According to the historical principles basic to Greek thought, Jewish law was the invention of Moses, enjoined by him upon his followers. If Menelaus now wished to impose his own law upon the people, his conduct could not be regarded as improper. It was these measures that passed into the consciousness of contemporaries and posterity as the "persecutions of Epiphanes." With them the history of the Maccabees begins.

JUDAH THE MACCABEE

———

Mattathias' following knew nothing of "historical necessity" and probably very little about the ideas of the reformers. The one thing plain to them was the fact of persecution: the Temple desecrated, the law abolished, and the Jews coerced into a pagan way of life. Against this persecution they defended themselves to the death. When, during 166 (or at the beginning of 165), Mattathias died, leadership devolved, we do not know why, upon the third of his living sons, Judah, surnamed the Maccabee. It is generally assumed that the surname signifies "hammer."

For two years Judah waged guerrilla war like his father, making surprise descents upon the apostates without venturing to attack any walled cities or the tyrant's stronghold in Jerusalem. Now he would appear at Beth Horon (about five hours northwest of Jerusalem), now at Modin, again at Mizpah, or at the Samaritan border. "And he was renowned unto the utmost part of the earth, and he gathered together those who were perishing."

At first the central government paid no attention whatsoever to the Maccabean uprising. It must be remembered that the Seleucid empire extended from Egypt to the Persian Gulf, and that disturbances of this nature flared up constantly at one point or another. The handful of the Maccabees could only be regarded as another robber band on the highways. But in the meanwhile Judah was steeling his company in guerrilla warfare. He also gave it a regular organization by appointing "captains of thousands, and captains of hundreds, and captains of fifties, and captains of tens." It would appear that his force amounted to something more than three thousand men.

It was important for the future course of events that the reform party made no attempt at mustering its strength to put an end, once and for all, to the activity of the marauders. Their failure is easy to understand if we reflect that they belonged to the upper strata of the people, being city dwellers and Jerusalemites, and did not particularly relish chasing after the Maccabees through gorges and over stony hills. The mass of the peasantry, on the other

113

hand, remained secretly devoted to the old faith. Judah ruthlessly extirpated the few in the country-side who followed the reform party, but at the same time he restored freedom of faith to the majority.

Before a battle Judah's company fasted, clothed themselves in sackcloth, rent their garments, and prayed devoutly to the Lord of Hosts: "Behold, the Gentiles are gathered together against us to destroy us. . . . How shall we be able to stand before them unless Thou help us?" Could so devout a prayer arise from the ranks of the reform party to the Zeus Olympius who was the creature of their reason? Surely not. Here, too, the reformers "halted between two opinions." It is significant that when they once sent an offering of money to the Tyrian Heracles, the consciences of the messengers were smitten and instead of using the money for what had been intended, they contributed it in Tyre to the construction of ships.

The new pagans of Jerusalem, the "sons of Acra," sought protection against Judah from the King's officers, whom they assisted moreover with auxiliaries, guides acquainted with the terrain, and the like. Judah defeated the troops that were sent against him, one after the other. When the Syrians were making a slow and laborious ascent to the pass

114

of Beth Horon along the mountain path that led from the coastal plain to Jerusalem, they were suddenly attacked by swarms of Maccabees, routed, and pursued the length of the slope into the lowland. Schooled by this defeat in the hills, another Syrian army took up a position in the plain near Emmaus. This afforded a convenient post for controlling the roads to Jerusalem. Judah made a halt near Mizpah in order to protect the road from Beth Horon to Jerusalem; during the night, under cover of the rough terrain, he led his company to a point south of Emmaus. The Syrian general planned to overwhelm the Maccabees by a surprise night attack. But while the King's troops were looking for Judah's forces in the hills, Judah made an attack at dawn upon the Syrian encampment at Emmaus. Later in the day, when the Syrian troops again approached Emmaus, they saw their camp in flames. They fled to the Philistine country.

The success of Judah can be more readily understood if we reflect upon the difficulties that guerrilla warfare in a hill country presents even to modern regular troops. The Seleucid armies were composed largely of contingents of auxiliaries from various cities and peoples; the professional soldiery was employed only for more important enterprises.

It was now, in the fall of 165, that Judah's successes began to disturb the central government. He appears to have controlled the road from Jaffa to Jerusalem, and thus to have cut off the royal party in Acra from direct communication with the sea and thus with the government. It is significant that this time the Syrian troops, under the leadership of the governor-general Lysias, took the southerly route, by way of Idumea. They encamped at Beth Zur, a fortress about thirty kilometers south of Jerusalem (whose remains have recently been excavated) that was the key to Judea from the south. This new tactic proved correct. Judah was forced to quit his hiding place in the hills and hurry southward. According to Jewish historical tradition, he then and there defeated Lysias. But certain other documents which happen to be preserved indicate that the situation was much more complicated than the Jewish historians represent it to have been. We see that the Maccabees sent deputies to Lysias to negotiate an understanding. Lysias promised to intercede for them with the King, if they would maintain their "good will towards the state." Menelaus, officiating High Priest and head of the reform party, intervened in the negotiations and appeared as mediator between the King and the Jews. A Roman embassy, probably en route to Antioch, took the Jews' part and persuaded them to formulate their demands quickly so that they themselves might present them to the King. Thus it appears that all parties were concerned to make peace between the government and the insurgents. In point of fact, Epiphanes was at the moment engaged in a serious war in the East, the imperial treasury was again empty, and the question of whether the Jews would eat in accordance with or in opposition to their dietary laws must now have seemed of little consequence to the government.

And so Epiphanes resolved to call a halt to the persecutions. In a proclamation to the Sanhedrin and the Jewish nation, he declared that he had been informed by Menelaus that the Jews who had fled from their homes—that is, those loyal to the ancient faith, amongst whom were the Maccabees—desired to return to their legal abodes. Exemption from punishment was guaranteed all who returned by March 29, 164 B.C.E., and in addition the assurance was given that the Jews would be permitted "to use their own food and to observe their own laws as of yore." The persecution was thus ended.

The edict makes no mention of the Maccabees, by as much as a syllable. It is represented as an act of

117

royal grace, instigated by Menelaus. But such an interpretation could not conceal the true state of affairs. The cessation of the persecutions signified the defeat of Menelaus, who had been their instigator, and the victory of the Maccabees—something that must have seemed unbelievable to contemporaries. David had again overcome Goliath. Only a year before the prophet Daniel could see no help except through a miraculous intervention of God. And yet Judah had won his victory with casual irregulars who were often lacking in such essential arms as sword and shield. How could the issue be interpreted as other than explicit confirmation of the leadership which the Maccabees had assumed?

From the beginning Judah comported himself as the lawful leader of his people. He put into force the law (Deut. 20:5-8) according to which a man who had built a house or betrothed a wife or planted a vineyard or was fainthearted was released from service. His people conscientiously separated first fruits and tithes, but these could only be offered in the Sanctuary, and the Sanctuary was still in the hands of the reform party. Epiphanes' restoration of freedom of conscience had only brought an end to the persecutions, but not to the rule of Menelaus and his friends. It was not to be expected that they would voluntarily surrender their position.

Judah therefore determined to wrest their rule from them by force. The tradition unfortunately leaves us in the dark as to where he and his people spent the summer of 164. It can be assumed that after the amnesty the majority of his men returned to their abandoned homes and fields. Hence it is probable that Judah re-enters history only toward the end of autumn, when work on the farm was finished.

At the end of 164, about the beginning of December, he again assembled "the entire host" and made a sudden descent upon Jerusalem. To understand that such a surprise attack could promise success, it must be remembered that in 168 the central government had pulled down Jerusalem's city walls; the intention was to make the city completely dependent upon the citadel of Acra. It was this that made it possible for Judah, only four years later, to take possession of Jerusalem so easily.

The first act of the conqueror was the purification of the Holy City of all traces of idolatry and the restoration of the service of God in the Temple. According to the Jewish calendar, it was Kislev 25, precisely

119

three years after the reform party had offered the first pagan sacrifice upon the altar, that Judah again carried out, in early morning, the prescribed Tamid sacrifice in the ancient usage. "And all the people fell upon their faces, and worshipped, and gave praise unto heaven, to him who had prospered them." For eight days the rededication of the purified altar was celebrated. Then "Judah and his brethren and the whole congregation of Israel ordained, that the days of the dedication of the altar should be kept in their seasons year by year for eight days, from the twenty-fifth day of the month Kislev, with gladness and joy." This celebration, which is the model for the annual festivals of dedication in all churches, is Hanukkah, a word that literally signifies "dedication." But this name can be documented only from the first century C.E. Originally the festival was called "Tabernacles (*Sukkot*) of the month of Kislev,"—so, for example, in an official communication from the Palestinian to the Egyptian Jews, dated 124 B.C.E.

By instituting this festival Judah and his people declared themselves the true Israel. Their act was one of far-reaching significance, for all previous festivals were prescribed in Scripture. Never had a festival been instituted in Israel by human hand.

Even the restoration of the Temple after the Babylonian Exile had not been solemnized by the establishment of a day of commemoration. Judah's measure was therefore an innovation without precedent. On the other hand, it was in complete accord with the usage of the Gentiles. Among the Greeks it was usual for a generation, when it regarded an event in its own history as important, to believe it should be commemorated for all time. Thus Judah imitated the practice of his enemies, but at the same time incorporated it into Judaism. This was the first step along the path which was to constitute the historic mission of the Hasmoneans—the introduction of Hellenic usages into Judaism without making a sacrifice of Judaism. No one any longer celebrates the Greek festivals that served as Judah's example. But the eight-branched candelabrum, a symbol, again, that imitates a pagan usage, is lighted on Kislev 25 the world over, in countries Judah never knew about, in Sydney as in New York, in Berlin as in Capetown. "And He saved them from the hand of him that hated them, and redeemed them from the hand of the enemy."

Master now of Jerusalem, Judah at once built high walls and strong towers about Mount Zion, quartered troops in the fortifications to protect the

Temple, and then fortified Beth Zur, which, as has been mentioned, protected the road to Jerusalem from the south. Thus, at the beginning of 163, Judah was master of Judea; only Acra remained as refuge and citadel for those loyal to the King.

We do not know why the group about Menelaus remained so inactive throughout this entire period. Apparently the garrison in Acra was too weak to act independently and the central government was, as usual, little concerned with the affairs of Judea. Moreover, at this time Epiphanes suffered a serious reverse in Persia when he attempted to plunder an Oriental sanctuary in the hill country, and was lying sick at Ispahan.

At the end of the winter of 163 B.C.E. Epiphanes died at Ispahan. About the same time Judah began the siege of Acra, already employing in this operation the best equipment of the great armies of that period, siege towers and battering-rams of various types. An unknown fugitive four years before, Judah was now, though without office or title, ruler over the Jewish nation. From Acra urgent dispatches went out to the central government. The reform party complained, with perfect justice, that the government was again leaving them, the group loyal to the King, in the lurch. "We were willing to serve thy father," the messengers said to the new king, Antiochus V Eupator, "and to walk after his words, and to follow his commandments. For this cause the children of our people besieged the citadel, and were alienated from us, and as many of us as they could light on they killed, and spoiled our inheritances."

At the head of the new government there stood as regent the same Lysias with whom Judah had negotiated a year previously and who had promised the Jews his good will if they would continue loyal. But in the meanwhile Judah had broken the peace and had taken advantage of the amnesty granted him to make himself master of Judea. The court at Antioch determined to dispose of the Maccabees once and for all.

In the summer of 163 Lysias himself marched at the head of an army of professional soldiers through Idumea to Jerusalem in order to raise the siege of Acra. His way was barred by the citadel of Beth Zur, which Judah had in the meanwhile occupied. Lysias directed the siege of this fortress, and Judah, obliged to hasten to the assistance of his outposts, was forced to interrupt the siege of Acra. This was Lysias' first success. Near Beth Zechariah, halfway between Jerusalem and Beth Zur, where the hills merge into a plateau that permits the deployment of larger battle formations, Judah one morning came upon Lysias' superior army, which included cavalry, and even thirty-two elephants, arms that were wholly wanting to the Maccabees. The rising sun was reflected in the gilt and brazen shields of the Syrian heavy infantry, so that "the mountains shone therewith, and blazed like torches of fire." Judah's brother, Eleazar, vainly immolating himself in an effort to save his people, rushed into the ranks of the enemy and attacked the largest of the elephants, upon which he naively supposed the young king to be riding. The beast, transfixed, fell, crushing the hero. Judah's army was defeated and Beth Zur capitulated.

The royal army now reached Jerusalem unhindered and laid siege to the fortified Mount Zion, where Judah and his people had taken refuge. In ancient times, before the use of explosives, every wall and every tower was an obstacle to the attacker. The besiegers therefore preferred to starve out rather than storm a besieged fortress. It was the summer of a Sabbath year, in which, according to biblical law, nothing had been planted. Hence there were no considerable supplies in Zion. Judah's troops dispersed, each man to his own home. Only a small company of the most faithful remained shut up in Zion under Judah's leadership. Judah's life was in any case forfeit. Moreover, we may surmise, he was firmly convinced that the God of Abraham, Isaac, and Jacob would not forsake him. In his desperate situation, therefore, Judah awaited a miracle, and the miracle came about. Expressed in untheological language, Judah's tenacity made it possible to expect a favorable turn in the situation, which, in the unforeseeable complications of life, might at any time take place.

The deliverance of the besieged Maccabees on Mount Zion came about as result of Epiphanes' last act on his deathbed in Persian Ispahan. When the King marched to the east he had left the guardianship of his son and successor, a minor, to Lysias, who after the death of the King assumed the regency. But on his deathbed Epiphanes had appointed another general, named Philip, as regent of his realm. And so it came about, approximately in February of 162, that while Lysias was occupied with the siege of Zion, he received word that Philip was approaching Antioch at the head of the army of the east to secure the overlordship for himself. Lysias found it necessary to withdraw in great haste, and so quickly made a peace with the beleaguered Judah.

Formally considered, the "peace" amounts on the

one hand to a capitulation on the part of Judah, and on the other, to a remission on the part of the King. In actuality, its basis was an understanding between Lysias and Judah which was tantamount to a restoration of the conditions that had obtained in Judea prior to Epiphanes. The King's remission was addressed to Lysias, and solemnly proclaimed renunciation of the policy of Epiphanes. "As for our Jewish subjects," the new King wrote, "we understand that they object to our father's project of bringing them over to Hellenism, preferring their own ways of life and asking permission to follow their own customs," and he was of the resolve "that the subjects of the realm should live undisturbed and attend to their own concerns." He agreed "to give them back their temple and to permit them to live after the manner of their ancestors."

A year earlier the government had consented to *tolerate* the Jewish religion; now the *dominion* of the Torah was fully restored. According to the decree of 163, those Jews who wished to do so might give obedience to the Jewish law. The new decree of 162 again obliged the entire people to observe this law. This marked the consummation of the victory of orthodox Judaism. For centuries thereafter the Jews celebrated the recurrence of this day (Shevat

28) "upon which King Antiochus withdrew from Jerusalem."

The consequences of the peace of 162 were twofold. For one thing, it marked the end of the reform party. Its chief, the former High Priest Menelaus, was executed upon the King's orders, "for that he was the cause of all the evil in that he persuaded Epiphanes to abolish the ancestral constitution of the Jews." This was the ground on which the verdict was based. The remaining partisans of reform, who continued to find refuge in the Acra, had in the meanwhile lost all touch with Judaism. The reformers had now become apostates.

On the other hand, the task of the Maccabees also seemed to have been completed. The government had deserted the reform party, traditional Judaism had been recognized as alone valid, and the conditions which had obtained before the promulgation of Epiphanes' measures were thus restored. The rebellion of the Jews now seemed pointless and at an end. "Now therefore let us give the right hand to these men, and make peace with them, and with all their nation; and let us settle with them that they be permitted to walk after their own laws, as aforetime; for because of their laws which we abolished were they angered, and did all these things." This

127

opinion of the young King's counselors proved correct. Judah was deserted by his partisans. The government appointed a new High Priest, a member of the previous high-priestly family called Jakim, who then Hellenized his name into Alcimus. The government even caused an assembly of scribes to be convoked so that it might confirm, after exhaustive investigation, that Alcimus was in fact the legitimate prince. The *Hasidim*, the "Pious," a group known for the strictness of its faith and who had been the first to join Mattathias, these very *Hasidim* were now the first to recognize Alcimus. From this time forward, supported by a royal guard, Alcimus ruled over Judea, and his power was so secure that he could without misgivings cause the execution of sixty of the "Pious" who had shown themselves rebellious. Once again the burnt offering for the reigning king was daily offered upon Zion.

At first Judah again retired into the mountains. But when a new revolution took place in Antioch—Antiochus V was overthrown by his cousin, Demetrius I—Judah took advantage of the occasion to reappear in Jerusalem. He took possession of the Sanctuary and even prevented Alcimus from approaching the altar. Judah's supporters maintained that Alcimus had "voluntarily polluted himself" in the time of Epiphanes; that is, without being compelled to do so, he had participated in pagan festivals and sacrifices. Was such a man now eligible to perform the service of God? The question was one of conscience, fought out by zealots and moderates, similar to the question which later arose among the early Christians during the time of persecutions: Can there be forgiveness for apostasy? We know that the various answers to this question led to numerous schisms within the Church and to reciprocal excommunications. It is therefore not surprising that Judah and his followers refused to recognize Alcimus, even after an assembly of sages convoked by the government had pronounced in favor of Alcimus' legitimacy.

This time the cleavage in the Jewish people was quite different from that in the days of Épiphanes. The struggle no longer concerned the validity of the Torah but whether or not Alcimus was justified in functioning as High Priest. As in the case of analogous divisions in the Church, the preponderant majority inclined to the latitudinarian view and recognized Alcimus. The former friends of the Maccabees were now transformed into enemies, "apostates." Civil strife began anew. Judah again marched forth. He swept through all the territory of Judea, taking vengeance upon his enemies and punishing the "apostates" who were worse than pagans in his eyes.

Twice Alcimus went to the royal court to request the government's help against the Maccabees, "who are keeping up the feud and stirring sedition; they will not let the kingdom settle down in peace." But Demetrius was entirely taken up with other difficulties, especially with the uprising of the satrap Timarchus, who, with Roman support, had wrested Mesopotamia from the King. Finally the King sent out one of his generals, Nicanor, with orders to take the Maccabees captive. Nicanor first sought to lay hands on Judah by cunning; but when the attempt miscarried, he marched his troops out of Jerusalem into the neighborhood of Beth Horon, where he was joined by troops from Syria. He himself led a levy of Jews loyal to the King out of Jerusalem. Because his troops were Jewish, he was constrained, much against his will, to abandon his intention of attacking Judah on the Sabbath. This was approximately in the month of March, 161 B.C.E.

The political situation had rapidly changed. It was only four years before that the government had punished the observance of the day of rest with death, and those wishing to hallow the Sabbath had sought help and refuge with Judah. Now they marched side by side with pagan soldiers in the attempt to capture Judah and send him to his death. At Adasa, northwest of Beth Horon, an hour and a half north of Jerusalem, where the road narrows as it passes through the hills, the opposing forces encountered one another. Judah's troops again proved far superior to the city levies. Nicanor fell on the field of battle and his army fled. Judah besieged Jerusalem and the Sanctuary a second time, and again had the day of his victory (Adar 13) entered in the calendar of festivals. This amounted to a demonstration that Judah and his followers represented the true Israel. For the first time in the history of Jacob a day in a war between brothers was declared a joyous festival. This example was later followed by the Pharisees, who upon occasion abused the function of festivals by instituting anti-Sadducee memorial days. All of these festivals, including the Day of Nicanor, have been forgotten. But the historian must point out that by instituting festivals of this nature Judah no less than the Pharisees was consciously or unconsciously imitating the example of the Greeks.

The victory over Nicanor in March 161 made Judah master of the country once again. He was not the only rebel in the empire. The prince of Greater Armenia, the governor of Commagene, and, above all, Timarchus, satrap of Media and Babylonia, had renounced their allegiance to King Demetrius I. These defections were facilitated by the Roman Senate, which refused to recognize Demetrius, supported his opponents, and finally concluded an alliance with Timarchus.

What did Judah know of Rome? The First Book of Maccabees represents him as having heard of the great reputation of the Roman people, "that they were valiant men, and that they were friendly disposed towards all who attached themselves to them, and that they offered friendship to as many as came unto them." That was enough for him. An exact knowledge of the details of a situation is often unnecessary, frequently even a hindrance, to resolute action. Judah knew that a Roman embassy had once before helped him (in 164 B.C.E.) ; he knew too that "whomsoever they will to succor and to make kings, become kings; and that whomsoever they will, do they depose." He therefore sent emissaries to Rome. They were well received and the Senate, which, as we have seen, was anxious to cause Demetrius I all possible difficulty, approved the treaty that was concluded, not, to be sure, with Judah and his brothers, but with the "nation of the Jews." "When the Jews rebelled against Demetrius I," an ancient historian writes, "and sought the friendship of Rome, they were the first of all Oriental peoples to receive a grant of freedom; the Romans were generous in disbursing what was not theirs." In any case, for the first time since the Exile the Jews were recognized as an independent power, and by the very people that ruled the world.

Christian theologians have often wondered at the fact that Judah, who was so zealous in the service of the Lord, made a treaty with and sought security through a pagan power, despite all the admonitions of the prophets. It must be said that there is ground for such wonder. The Maccabees had again taken a step that brought them nearer to the pagan world; they had again accommodated devout Judaism to the ways of the nations.

It may be argued that the Roman alliance, which was Judah's greatest success, became the immediate cause of his downfall. The Seleucid government could look on calmly at the occasional successes of a guerrilla chief, in expectation of a favorable moment for delivering a blow. But when Judah became a protégé of Rome, it seemed essential to act at once. Judah's emissaries returned to Jerusalem towards the end of the summer of 161. In the first month of the following spring, as soon as the rainy season was ended, the King's general Bacchides, accompanied by Alcimus and at the head of a regular army, moved through Galilee towards Jerusalem. As always, the professional soldiers were qualitatively far superior to the Maccabean irregulars. When the Syrians approached, the greater part of the Maccabean levy, which amounted to three thousand men, fled. Only eight hundred remained with Judah, and "he was sore troubled in heart." Friends advised him to avoid the battle, and their counsel was undoubtedly strategically sound. But he preferred death in battle, and fell fighting. "All Israel made great lamentation for him and mourned many days, and said: 'How is the mighty one fallen, the savior of Israel!' "

Israel quickly forgot Judah. In the Talmud he is nowhere mentioned. In *Megillat Antiochus,* a post-talmudic (and quite spiritless) account that was read at the Hanukkah festival in the Middle Ages, Mattathias and his grandson, John Hyrcanus—but not Judah—are the principal figures. It was only during the Middle Ages, thanks to the Hebrew compilation called *Josippon,* composed on the basis of the writings of Josephus, that Judah again became a hero for the Jews. The Christian world, which had taken the Books of Maccabees into their Holy Scripture, meanwhile honored Judah as a paragon of knighthood. Even today the statue of Judah may be seen in the principal market place of Nuremberg. His figure, along with those of eight other heroes (three pagans, three Jews, three Christians), decorates the *Schöne Brunnen* (1385), a masterpiece of the age of chivalry.

———

Judah fell in April 160 B.C.E. After his death "the lawless put forth their heads in all the borders of Israel, and all they that wrought iniquity rose up." The partisans of Judah were tracked down everywhere and large numbers were executed. A system of garrisoning instituted by the Syrians provided for the peace and order of the country. Jonathan, Judah's brother and successor, again became the simple chief of a band, and sought refuge now in the wilderness of Tekoa and now in Trans-Jordan. Not much more can be told of his deeds during this period than an attack upon an Arab wedding procession to avenge the death of his brother John. Finally, about 156, he grew weary of the life of an outlaw. He too made his peace with the government, gave hostages for his good conduct, and received Michmash, a place west of Jericho, as his place of residence. Here "he began to judge the people," that is to say, he was recognized by the government as sheik of the village. In ancient times, and even later,

136

this was the lot that many an Oriental leader of a troop earned in the decline of his life; in this way he was assured a secure benefice. "And the sword ceased from Israel."

Eight years elapsed after the death of Judah before the Maccabees again entered history. It was the Syrians who aroused Jonathan from his slumbers in Michmash. In 152 B.C.E. a pretender called Alexander Balas arose against the reigning king, Demetrius I, the conqueror of Judah. Alexander Balas landed at Acco and its garrison went over to him. Demetrius was in great straits, for the Roman Senate had recognized Alexander, and the kings of Egypt, Pergamum, and Cappadocia supported him. This made it extremely difficult, if not impossible, for Demetrius to obtain soldiers abroad. The King required reliable troops immediately. What could be more natural than to turn to his warlike Jewish subjects and there enlist the necessary warriors? Twenty centuries ago the highland Jews of Palestine were rough peasants and shepherds who had grown up in an inhospitable country; they were known for their boldness and ruthlessness in war, and like the Arabs they terrified neighboring agricultural countries by their inroads. As soon as they gained a footing on the coast under Jonathan, we find pirates among them. All in all, they were excellent soldiers, loyal to their oath of fealty, whose only inconvenience was their numerous "superstitions," as for example the apparently stupid custom of observing complete rest every seventh day, a habit whose purpose no Greek was able to fathom.

But an inexcusable blunder on the part of the central government had left Jewry at this juncture with no legitimate prince. After the death of Alcimus in the spring of 159, no successor had been named. There was only one man who commanded sufficient authority among the Jews to muster an army for Demetrius I. This was Jonathan, Judah's brother and heir. Demetrius gave Jonathan full power to collect troops.

Jonathan naturally used the opportunity first to secure his own position—he occupied Jerusalem and fortified Zion anew. Syrian garrisons continued only in Acra and in Beth Zur. Naturally, too, Alexander Balas now sought to draw the Jewish leader over to his side. Jonathan demanded his price, and it was given him. At the Feast of Tabernacles in 152 B.C.E. he clothed himself, by the authority of Alexander Balas, in the sacred vestments of the High Priest.

Judah had fought bitterly against the High Priest Alcimus because he was "polluted." Eight years later Jonathan raised himself to the position of High Priest, despite the fact that he was not a member of the Zadokite family to which the office appertained. For the priest to obtain his position from the secular power was a Greek custom. Once again those who fought for the Torah accommodated the law to Gentile practices, while the legitimate High Priest (by right of descent) performed the service in a rump temple in Egypt.

Jonathan's fantastic rise in the few months of the autumn of 152 B.C. from petty chieftain to High Priest of the Temple in Jerusalem and prince in Israel ushers in a chapter in the history of the Maccabees which, except for the identity of the family, has little in common with the previous course of their destiny. Judah's lifework had been to prevent the threatening Hellenization of Judaism and the surrender of the Torah. He succeeded, and gave his life to his success. Jonathan and his successors, his brother Simon and Simon's descendants, will now seek to accommodate Hellenism to Judaism. Under them Judea becomes a Hellenistic principality.

This development began with Jonathan's becoming involved in international politics. Perhaps this involvement was at first a matter of necessity. As prince of Judea he was forced to choose among the pretenders who throughout his entire reign competed for the crown of Syria. But this meant that for the first time since the destruction of the First Temple and the Babylonian Exile (586) Judea became an active member of the family of nations.

Jonathan's first task was to maintain himself. This required that he watch the political currents and keep in touch with the pagan princes; but it also meant that he had to sacrifice the blood of Jews for the cause of one or the other of the pretenders. He became a Seleucid official, a *strategos* and governor of a province; he received a court title and wore the purple reserved for the "friends of the king." At one time he sent the government three thousand men to suppress an insurrection in Antioch. They set the city on fire, slew everyone who fell into their hands, and plundered at will. It can be imagined with what relish these peasants and shepherds pillaged the pagan city.

Jonathan's second endeavor was to secure his position in Jerusalem. He had many enemies in Judea, of course, who took every opportunity to complain of him to the government. The Greek city of Acra and its citadel remained a constant threat to his rear. At one time he sought to take it by force, another time to negotiate for it with the government. But the kings in Antioch, as soon as they came to power, held fast to this stronghold by which they were able to control Jonathan.

Finally he proceeded to round out the boundaries of his principality; it is significant that what he sought first of all was access to the sea. His brother, who also obtained official preferment and was promoted to the governorship of the (at that time) non-Jewish coastal region, took advantage of the opportunity to place a Jewish garrison in the pagan city of Jaffa, in order to forestall the city's going over to a pretender to the throne.

It is superfluous to describe in this place the campaigns and political combinations in which Jonathan, and after his death his brother and successor, Simon, engaged. (Jonathan was taken captive and murdered at the end of 143 by a Syrian pretender.) They fought battles as *condottieri* now of one and now of another of the Seleucids against their opponents, and always found a reason to shift their allegiance as circumstances demanded. Meanwhile they strengthened the position of their house in Judea. Thus they succeeded in getting into their power all important fortresses, such as Beth Zur, Gezer, and, finally, Acra in Jerusalem—this last on Iyar 23 (about May) 141. During the same period and by the same means, veering between kings and counterkings, many other leaders succeeded in establishing principalities in Syria.

But in two respects the work of Jonathan and of Simon was different from that of their rivals. For one thing, they preceded the others, who came up in the following generation. Next, and in particular, the Maccabees not only established their personal authority but also extended the power of their people. The basis of their rule was national, or more properly, religious. When Simon won Gezer or Acra, he expelled the pagan inhabitants, purified the place of "pollution," and settled it with Jews.

The results of Jonathan's and Simon's activity may accordingly be summarized somewhat as follows: In 152, when Jonathan was installed as High Priest, the boundaries of Judea were the Jordan and the Dead Sea on the east; the meridian of Modin (approximately) on the west; Beth Horon and Bethel to the north; and in the south, Beth Zur. Jonathan added to this three districts of southern Samaria, and also Lydda and Ekron. Simon acquired the great plain, the seacoast from Jaffa to Ascalon, and Hebron in the south. In fifteen years the extent of the area subject to Jerusalem was approximately doubled; not only the hill country but the fertile plain now became Jewish and Jerusalem was provided with its harbors.

Their political success consisted in the emancipation of the Jews from the rule of the Seleucids. In May 142 Simon obtained Israel's complete freedom from tribute. "Therefore was the yoke of the heathen taken away from Israel." Public documents began to be dated according to the years of Simon. A year later the Hellenistic city and the citadel in Jerusalem, Acra, was taken. In the year 139 Simon received the royal privilege of striking (copper) coins in his own name. On Elul 18 (about September) of the preceding year (140 B.C.E.) "in a great congregation of priests and people and princes of the nation, and of the elders of the country," it was determined that Simon should be "their leader and High Priest for ever." Heretofore the legal basis for the power of the Maccabean princes had been royal appointment. Now the rule of Simon and of his successors rested upon the decision of the people itself; hence Simon assumed the new title, "Prince of the People" (Ethnarch). But lest the people in its fickleness change its mind, it was also resolved that no one should be permitted to alter this law or to convoke assemblies without Simon's consent.

These various successes the Jews owed not so much to their own strength as to the adroitness of their leaders, Jonathan the "Sly" (so is his nickname *Aphphus* probably to be interpreted) and his brother, the Ethnarch Simon. Jonathan and Simon made their conquests as *condottieri* of the pretenders to the Syrian throne, whose partisans threw the gates of the rebellious cities open to them. Only in such a manner was it possible for Jonathan, for example, to subjugate a city like Gaza—which would ordinarily have required a siege of years—merely by devastating the surrounding countryside. This signified only that the city had attached itself to King Antiochus VI, who was represented by Jonathan, and not at all that it had surrendered to the Jews. Although Jonathan and Simon after him continued to hold the cities they had won, garrisoning them for security, it was clear that as soon as the dynastic struggles of the Seleucids ended they would have to restore their conquests to their legitimate suzerains. Jonathan and Simon gambled on the wars of the pretenders never ending. On the whole, they were quite right, but a temporary consolidation of Seleucid power nevertheless robbed the Maccabees of their gains, and forced John Hyrcanus, the son and successor of Simon, to revolutionize the foreign policy of his house and hence also the internal structure of the princedom.

In the year 139 there appeared a new pretender in Syria, Antiochus VII Sidetes, son of that Demetrius I who had crushed the insurrection of Judah the Maccabee. Antiochus was forced to wage war against Tryphon, a general who had proclaimed himself king and had removed the former ruler, Antiochus VI, an illegitimate grandson of Epiphanes.

While yet upon his way to Syria, Antiochus VII confirmed all of Simon's former privileges and in addition granted him the right to strike coins of small denomination "for thy country with thine own stamp." But when he arrived in Syria he immediately made a demand upon Simon either to surrender the cities outside Judea, such as Jaffa and Gezer, and, significantly, Acra in Jerusalem, or to make a single payment of a thousand talents of silver in compensation. Simon replied: "We have neither taken other men's land, nor have we possession of that which appertaineth to others, but of the inheritance of our fathers; howbeit, it was had in possession of our enemies wrongfully for a certain time. But we, having the opportunity, hold fast the inheritance of our fathers." Only for Jaffa, which had never been Jewish, and for Gezer did he offer compensation, in the sum of a hundred talents. Thus, though his argument was not wholly consistent, he opposed an historical claim to the land of his fathers to the King's title in law.

Antiochus VII was occupied with the campaign against Tryphon and so at first was able only to dispatch one of his officers as commander of the coastal area to prevent further expansion on the part of the Jews. His general Cendebaieus made Jabneh his base of operations and built the fortress of Kedron (now the village Katra) between Jabneh and Ashdod. From these bases he made incursions into Jewish territory; these were met more or less successfully by the Maccabees, and avenged by counterincursions. It was not until the summer of 134, after the death of Simon (who was murdered in February by his own son-in-law), that Antiochus VII personally led his army against Jerusalem, where in the meantime John (Yohanan) Hyrcanus, the son and heir of Simon, had assumed the rule. As always, the Jewish levy broke down in the face of the professional army of the King. By November Antiochus stood before Jerusalem and directed its siege. A double trench now cut off Jerusalem from all approach. Following a customary practice in ancient sieges, Hyrcanus expelled noncombatants from the Holy City in order to reduce the number of mouths that had to be fed. For the same reason Antiochus sent them back, and they wandered back and forth between the two armies. It was not until the Feast of Tabernacles in the fall of 133 that Hyrcanus received them back into the city. He also requested a seven days' truce of Antiochus because of the festival. Antiochus consented and even sent sacrificial animals, which were naturally wanting in the beleaguered city. In this manner negotiations were initiated. Hyrcanus was forced to capitulate. In the negotiations, however, the King confirmed the autonomy of the Jews and the position of Hyrcanus; but the walls of Jerusalem were pulled down. Hyrcanus was required to provide hostages, pay tribute, and yield up all the conquests of the Maccabees outside Judea. Even Gezer was taken from him. In 130 he was required to accompany the King upon his Parthian campaign with a Jewish levy. The achievement of Jonathan and Simon seemed to have been destroyed at a single blow. Jerusalem was again a dependent city, as in the days of Epiphanes and Demetrius I. But now the High Priest was not of the legitimate house, but was a grandson of that Mattathias who, thirty years previously, had begun the insurrection against the great-uncle of Antiochus VII.

JOHN HYRCANUS

———

Antiochus VII fell in his Parthian campaign (129 B.C.E.). A new epoch of confusion in the succession began in the Seleucid empire. The pretenders were now entirely without authority; each city and each tyrant pursued his own policy. The period of veering and tacking, the period of the tactics of Jonathan and Simon, was at an end. Upon the throne of the Maccabees now sat the representative of a new generation, John Hyrcanus, whose Greek name was apparently Alexander. He was born after the period of the persecutions; it was later thrown up to him that his mother had been a war captive under Epiphanes, and that her marriage to the priest Simon had therefore not been permissible. He was only a child when his uncle Jonathan became High Priest in the fall of 152. That he would obtain power was thus for him a foregone conclusion. Under his father he had been governor of Gezer. But the religious war, the struggle against the reform party, the hatred of the Greek oppressor—all that had inspired the sons of Mattathias, despite everything, to the end of their days—seemed to him strange and remote.

John Hyrcanus became a Hellenistic prince like his contemporaries and rivals, Zeno Cotylas in Rabbath Ammon (modern Amman) in Trans-Jordan, Erotimus, King of the Nabateans, and others. Each of them strove to expand his domain without troubling in the least about the Seleucids. Hyrcanus too became fully independent of the Seleucids; "Neither as subject nor as friend did he yield them aught." Unlike his uncle and his father, Hyrcanus wished to stand entirely upon his own feet.

But for this the first requisite was an effective army. The Jewish levy was as incompetent in the plain—particularly against the professional armies recruited from the Grecized cities of the coast—as it was superior in its native hills. How were these primitively armed Jewish shepherds to stand against the heavily armed horse and foot of the professional armies when the scene of battle was transferred to the level country "where there is neither stone nor flint, nor any place to flee unto"? But John wished to regain the plain and the coastal regions which he had lost in the peace pact of 133, and now there was no pretender to the throne whose protection could open the gates of the Greek cities to him. He had to organize a professional army, and that meant that he must recruit foreign soldiers. Immediately after the peace of 133, so it is said, in order to procure funds to hire mercenaries he opened the tomb of David and removed the treasures allegedly hidden there. This put an end to the popular period of the Maccabean monarchy. The prince now possessed an armed force alien to the people and obedient to him alone.

With these mercenaries, supplemented, of course, by native levies, Hyrcanus succeeded within twenty-five years in raising Judea to the position of the most significant military power in Syria. The course of his conquests is little known. He may have suffered frequent setbacks. We learn from two Roman documents of the period, for example, that in 132 the Jews sought Roman intervention to procure the restoration "of Jaffa, the harbors [that is, the landing places between Jabneh and Gaza], Gezer, Pegae, and other of their cities and localities which Antiochus had taken by force of arms contrary to the decree of the Senate." The reference was to the war against Antiochus VII. But about 110 we find them again complaining in Rome that Antiochus IX "had

taken their fortresses and harbors and land." Soon
Hyrcanus succeeded in winning back these "harbors," and the Jews besought the Roman Senate for
protection "for their land and their harbors."

All this makes it plain how spirited was the struggle between the Jews and their opponents for access
to the Mediterranean. At the turn of the century, in
any case, the Jews were firmly established on the
coast. Hyrcanus' realm extended as far north as Carmel. He was able to subjugate the hated Samaritans,
and destroyed their temple on Mount Gerizim. Galilee was incorporated in the princedom and assigned
as residence to Alexander Jannaeus, the younger son
of Hyrcanus. In the south the Idumeans were sub-
jugated. They accepted circumcision and the Torah
and soon became complete Jews. When Hyrcanus
died he left his son and successor, Judah Aristobulus, a territory which stretched from the north of
Galilee to Masada, and from the sea to the Jordan.

Aristobulus reigned for only one year (104 to
103), and was succeeded by his brother, Alexander
Jannaeus. Jannaeus continued his father's policy
and waged incessant war against the neighboring
cities and princes. At his death (76 B.C.E.) the entire
coast, with the exeeption of Ascalon, from the border
of Egypt to Carmel was under his sway. He won

Trans-Jordan, which at that time contained numerous flourishing Greek settlements. "The land between Gaza and Lebanon is called Judea," wrote a Greek geographer of the time. Palestine, "from Dan to Beersheba," was Jewish again. The biblical prophecies of happiness and prosperity seemed to have been fulfilled. But they were realized after Judea had become a Hellenistic princedom, and, after Aristobulus, a Hellenistic kingdom. It was this that provided the strength with which to conquer, but it was also this that was the inward reason for the dissolution of the new realm.

———

Today it is possible for us to observe the process of
Hellenization in individual features only. But these
features are sufficiently significant to enable those
who wish and are able to do so, to grasp the unity
of the historical reality.

A first indication of "assimilation" is the accommodation of proper names to the taste of the surrounding world. The leaders of the reform party
called themselves Jason instead of Jeshu, Menelaus
instead of Onias; the real name of the High Priest
Alcimus was Jakim. The Maccabees, on the other
hand, bore purely Hebrew names. Mattathias, son
of Yohanan, son of Simon, called his children
Yohanan (John), Simon, Judah, Eleazar, Jonathan.
His companions in the struggle were called Joseph,
Azariah, Mattathias, Judah. When emissaries were
to be sent to Rome, to be sure, they had to be persons
fluent in Greek, and they bore such names as Jason

and Eupolemus. But already Simon's son-in-law was called Ptolemaeus, and the sons of John Hyrcanus, Simon's grandson, had double names, Aristobulus-Judah, Alexander Jannaeus (*Yannay,* a short form of Jonathan). John Hyrcanus and Aristobulus struck their coins only in Hebrew; Jannaeus' coins are bilingual, bearing "King Jonathan" in Hebrew and "King Alexander" in Greek.

These coins were struck about 100 B.C.E. But forty years earlier, when the struggle with the Seleucids was still being waged, the Maccabees, who are customarily regarded as the bitter enemies and destroyers of Hellenistic culture, proclaimed the adherence of the Jewish people to the Hellenistic world. This took place in 143, under the High Priest Jonathan.

From the time of Alexander the Great, Greeks had been masters of the East. It was natural that the peoples and tribes of the East endeavored, by means of more or less skilfully contrived genealogical constructions, to attach themselves to the Greek people and to profess a kinship with them. Such a connection constituted, as it were, a ticket of admission to European culture. Thus, for example, the Pisidian city of Selge and the Lydian settlement of Cibyra in Caria, both mixed "barbarian" settlements in south-west Asia Minor, declared themselves to be Spartan colonies. In the year 126-125 Phoenician Tyre officially informed the Delphians of their kinship with them. Such derivations were promoted and facilitated by the tendencies of Greek science to link all new peoples, more or less naively, with those already known. The medieval practice of fitting newly discovered races into the framework of the biblical roll of nations (Gen. 10) is analogous. On the basis of an ingenious combination Greek scholarship had contrived a connection between the Jews and the Spartans. This was known as early as about 170 B.C.E. When Jason, the leader of the reform party, was ousted by Menelaus, he fled to Sparta and there claimed hospitality on the grounds of tribal kinship.

But as soon as the Maccabee Jonathan, who had so unexpectedly risen to be High Priest and chief of Jewry, was firmly in the saddle, he sent an embassy to Sparta (about 143) to renew the ancestral bond of brotherhood. His missive to "his brother Spartans" is extant. In it Jonathan refers to a letter of a Spartan king to "Onias the High Priest," and he subjoins a copy of this letter. The Spartan letter is a patent forgery, fabricated by some writer in Jonathan's service. In the spirit of the cosmopolitan

155

philosophy of the period the Spartans are represented as saying to the Jews: "Your cattle and your possessions are ours, and ours are yours." But most important, the alleged Spartan declares that "in a writing concerning the Spartans and the Jews, the statement is made that they are brothers and, indeed, of the race of Abraham."

The forgery is not very skilful, but it is perfectly consonant with the spirit of the time. Men were eager to "discover" ancient evidence as a basis for the most recent friendships. But in all the forgeries and fictions of this class it is always the barbarians who claim a Hellenic descent: Romulus, the founder of Rome, is descended from Aeneas, a hero of the Iliad. It is significant of the Jewish forgery that the relationship is reversed: the Spartans are connected with the biblical patriarch.

Here the character and significance of Maccabean Hellenism is plainly revealed. The reform party wished to assimilate the Torah to Hellenism; the Maccabees wished to incorporate Hellenic culture in the Torah. The process was like that of the Europeanization of Japan: Japan possessed scholars who wrote about Botticelli and scientists who made bacteriological discoveries, but at the same time it could proclaim the Mikado's divine right of sovereignty

156

on the ground of his direct descent from the goddess of the sun.

This accommodation of new elements to the Bible, this consideration for native tradition, characterizes the Hellenization carried through under the Maccabees, and differentiates it from the rationalistic assimilation which had been the aim of the reform party. Let us consider, for example, the decree of 140 B.C.E., by which the people invested Simon with the rulership. The document is thoroughly Hellenistic in character. It must have been drafted in Greek. In any case, the form is altogether that of a Greek honorary decree, utterly impossible in Hebrew. A long-winded and awkward period sets forth the reasons for the decree, and the decree itself is then expressed in an appended sentence. The very notion of drawing up a document to establish a constitution is purely Greek; the Bible provides no pattern for this. According to Hebrew models one would expect a general obligation of the people to Simon by means of an oath. But in this very document, which prohibits the wearing of purple or of the gold brooch which are the insignia of Hellenistic royalty, which offers Simon the rule out of gratitude for his deeds and in which he accepts it, a sharp distinction is nevertheless drawn between the privileged priesthood and the people; and rule is secured to Simon with the limitation, "until a faithful prophet shall arise." Only a divine revelation, not an assembly of the people, could proclaim eternal law for Israel.

Let us glance for a moment at Jonathan's letter to the Spartans. It is his desire to make known the kinship of the Jews with this Greek people. But at the same time he emphasizes that "the holy Scriptures we possess bring comfort to the Jews, and the help of Heaven delivers the Jews out of the hand of their enemies." Naively, he informs the Spartans that the Jews will remember them in their prayers, "as proper duty requires that brothers be remembered." We may imagine that the Spartans were somewhat puzzled by this missive. Their reply contains only a diplomatically courteous acknowledgment.

A third example. In antiquity as today, a proper legal title was sought for every conquest. Greek opinion held that the original legitimate owners of a territory might maintain a permanent claim upon it if it had been wrested from them by force. Thus the opponents of the Maccabees in the Greek cities of Phoenicia and Palestine maintained at the time of the Maccabean conquest that the Jews could have no claim upon Palestine because they were immigrants who had destroyed the Canaanites: "Are ye not a people of robbers?" It is of the highest significance for the Hellenization of Judaism under the Maccabees that the Jews engaged in this dispute without objection, that is to say, they recognized Greek opinion as arbiter in the case. Thus, it is important to note, they accepted the legal principle of their opponents. Whereas the Bible eschews any secular legal basis for the claim upon the land and derives the Jews' right to Canaan from the divine promise, under the Maccabees the Jews sought a historical basis for their claim to the Holy Land. But, and this is characteristic of the manner of their Hellenization, they applied this new principle to the Bible. They declared, for example, that Palestine originally belonged to the heritage of Shem and had then been occupied by Canaan in robber-fashion; or they identified Shem with Melchizedek, the priest-king of Jerusalem, thus seeking to prove that Palestine was Shem's heritage; or they employed some similar device. But it did not occur to them, for instance, to follow the Greek historian Hecataeus and dismiss all the charges of their opponents with the claim that Palestine was completely uninhabited at the time of the Jewish immigration. In territorial

159

disputes of this nature the Greeks always cited the writings of the historians, ancient documents, and similar sources, or even Homer; if one party to a quarrel found that some passage in the document to which it was appealing did not suit its argument, it declared that the offending passage had been interpolated. The Jews took over the Greek manner of argumentation, but for them the only source of knowledge remained the sacred Scripture, even when its evidence was against them.

The accommodation of Hellenistic civilization to the Torah, begun by the Maccabees and carried forward under their rule, gave Judaism the form that it was to have for centuries and that, in part, prevailed until the Emancipation. Judaism of the post-Maccabean period is Pharisaic. But Pharisaism, which is first mentioned in the period of John Hyrcanus, who was a disciple of the Pharisees, is in part characterized precisely by the introduction of certain leading ideas of the Hellenistic period into the world of the Torah.

The Pharisees or *perushim*, as they are designated in Hebrew, are the "Separated" who stand apart from the pagans and also from other Jews in order to gain sanctity. For them *parush* becomes a synonym for *kadosh*, "holy." They are not the only ones who separated themselves. The Essenes, another sect, who seem to have introduced something of the ideas and the forms of life of Greek Pythagoreanism into Judaism, desired to be "holy" no less than the Pharisees, and their striving in this direction was even more pronounced than the Pharisees'. But the Essenes sought to realize their goal for themselves alone, for the members of their own order; the Pharisees, on the other hand, wished to embrace the whole people, and in particular through education. It was their desire and intention that everyone in Israel achieve holiness through the study of the Torah, and their guiding principle was: "Raise up many disciples."

All of this is alien to biblical Israel. The prophets looked forward to repentance as issuing from the pressure of events and as a result of prophetic admonitions and divine chastisement, not as the fruit of study. Even for Jesus Sirach, who wrote his Book of Wisdom on the eve of the persecutions of Epiphanes, the scholar is a distinguished man and a rich one. An artisan or peasant, in his view, could not attain learning. "He that hath little business," he says, "can become wise. How can he become wise that holdeth the goad?" But the Pharisees wished to bring everyone to the Torah. "The crown of the

Torah is set before every man." For Sirach, as for biblical Judaism, as indeed for all the East, it is assumed that only the pious can be wise: "All wisdom cometh from the Lord." The Pharisees adopted this principle entirely, adding to it, however, that piety was teachable and to be attained only through teaching. Consequently the entire people must study the Torah.

But this is a Hellenic, one might say, a Platonic notion, that education could so transform the individual and the entire people that the nation would be capable of fulfilling the divine task set it. Hellenism introduces the first epoch of general popular education in the Occident. The Hellenes and the Grecized Orientals assembled in the gymnasia that were everywhere to be found and that served at once as athletic fields, schools, and clubs. In late Hellenistic Alexandria, as in the Greek community of the reform party in Jerusalem, the rights of citizenship were granted only after a sort of "proficiency test" was passed.

The Pharisees adopted these ideas and tendencies of the Hellenistic world, in that they associated the public sermons that had been customary since the time of Ezra with the teaching of the Torah. But it was not their ideal to fashion a Greek *kalos kai*

162

agathos, or "gentleman," but to fulfil the precept which introduces the revelation on Sinai: "Ye shall be unto Me a kingdom of priests, and a holy nation."

To become a holy nation, indeed, was a goal common to all the Jews. But the Pharisees differed from the others by seeking its achievement through education and by not limiting this education to the Torah of Moses; they added many precepts wanting in the Torah, as, for example, the rule of washing the hands before meat. Any law written down naturally needs to be added to, and affords room for interpretation. One sect of Judaism in the Maccabean period, the Sadducees, wished to limit the laws to those expressly contained in the Torah. If something was neither prescribed nor forbidden in the Torah, they did not wish to make it so. Their principle was: "Only what is written is authoritative." But the Pharisaic idea of education promoted the tendency to develop the Torah as time and circumstance demanded. As the source for such development, the Pharisees looked to tradition, or, as they later termed it, the "oral" law, which they set on a footing with the written Torah. This singular notion of setting traditional usage or *halakhah* alongside the written law is again Greek. It is the concept of the "unwritten law" (*agraphos nomos*), which is preserved

163

not on stone or paper but lives and moves in the actions of the people. But whereas in the Greek world this notion often served to negate the written law, Pharisaism used the oral law to "make a fence for the Torah."

In this way Maccabean Hellenism succeeded in parrying spiritual movements which might otherwise have destroyed traditional Judaism. For example, the Hellenistic world surrounding Judaism was caught up by a new revelation that solved the problem of evil on earth: retribution would come after death, when the wicked would be punished and the righteous rewarded and awakened to new life. Such notions are alien to the Bible, indeed in contradiction to it, for the Torah promises reward and punishment in this life. Hence the Sadducees rejected the new doctrine and ridiculed the Pharisaic teaching of resurrection. If they had been the only authoritative representatives of Judaism, Judaism would either have lagged behind the times and grown rigid, as was the case with the Samaritans, who also rejected the new belief, or the course of history would have submerged Judaism and undermined the Torah. The Pharisees, on the other hand, adopted the Hellenistic doctrine of resurrection, but subsumed it under the principles of the Torah.

What to the pagans was an event dictated more or less by necessity, appears among the Jews as the working of the free will of God. According to the account of Flavius Josephus, the Pharisaic doctrine of the future life derives from the Greek teaching of the Pythagoreans. But among the Pythagoreans each soul must automatically return to new life after death, each according to its merit. For this fateful and continually operative necessity, the Pharisees substituted the single event of the Last Judgment, whose day and scope God would determine, and so dovetailed the new Hellenistic idea into the structure of biblical ideas. In its new form the adopted doctrine of resurrection developed into a characteristic element of Jewish belief; it became, with biblical monotheism, its central doctrine. The Jewish prayer book still reads: "Praised be Thou, Lord our God and God of our fathers, God of Abraham, God of Isaac, and God of Jacob. . . . Thou art mighty for eternity, O Lord, Thou quickenest the dead."

———

The Pharisees wished to make over the entire people
of Israel into their own image—they wished to make
of Israel, as the command on Sinai prescribed, "a
holy nation." In consequence, they came forward
with such comprehensive claims as no party either
before or after them had done. In the house as upon
the street, every movement of the pious was regu-
lated. The Pharisees prescribed that no knot might
be tied or loosed on the Sabbath, but they also prescribed the cases in which this rule might admit of
exceptions. For example, a woman might tie the
strings of her bonnet on a Saturday. So comprehensive a concept of the life of a people is only possible when and because the people are in full agreement with the dominant belief. At the time of Flavius
Josephus—that is to say, at the time of the destruction of the Temple by the Romans (70 c.e.)—the

spiritual unity of party and people had been attained. Although the Pharisees had no constitutional means of enforcing discipline, Josephus tells us, they possessed such influence that the people concurred with them even when they spoke against King or High Priest. All acts of worship, prayers as well as sacrifices, were carried out according to their ordinances. Even the Sadducees, whenever they obtained official positions, were obliged to keep to what the Pharisees laid down, however irksome and constraining they might find it, for otherwise they would not be tolerated by the people. It was about the year 100 that the Pharisees made their bid for spiritual domination over Israel, and their comprehensive claims necessarily developed into a conflict with the Maccabees. The ideal state, Plato declared, cannot come into being unless kings become philosophers or philosophers kings. The Pharisees were confronted with the same dilemma: the Maccabees must either become Pharisees or give way to the Pharisees.

According to our sources, the vicissitudes of the conflict between the state and the religious movement developed somewhat as follows: John Hyrcanus (134 to 104) was at first a friend and disciple of the Pharisees. He permitted them to lay their commands and prohibitions upon the people. Later he turned from them, allegedly because he was personally offended by a Pharisee. "He forbade observance of their regulations on pain of punishment, and joined the Sadducees. In consequence the hatred of the people was turned upon him and his sons."

The Pharisees of the period of 100 B.C.E. must not be imagined according to the pattern of the peace-loving teachers of Jabneh who were preaching harmony two centuries later. Early Pharisaism was a belligerent movement that knew how to hate.

When Alexander Jannaeus was defeated by the Arabs about 90 B.C.E. he fled to Jerusalem. This military reverse, as is often the case, afforded the enemies of the government opportunity to agitate. Civil strife began, and lasted for six years. When Jannaeus asked the insurgents what they wished, they replied, his death. Against this great-grandson of Mattathias they invited the assistance of one of the last of the Seleucids, Demetrius III. The armies met at Shechem. Demetrius urged Jannaeus' mercenaries to make common cause with him, the Hellene; and Jannaeus, for his part, sought to move the Jews who were with Demetrius to desert. Demetrius won. Jannaeus' mercenaries were annihilated. But sympathy for the defeated Jews caused a portion of Demetrius' Jewish allies to desert the pagan victor. Demetrius retired from the country and Jannaeus was enabled to suppress the insurrection. In Jerusalem he celebrated his triumph in a carousal with his concubines. In their presence he set up eight hundred crosses on which to nail the captive rebels, whose wives and children were slaughtered before their eyes.

It is not easy to determine whether the insurrection was the work of the Pharisees or whether other elements exploited for their own purposes the dissatisfaction fanned by the Pharisees. A pregnant sentence of Jannaeus' is preserved in the Talmud: "Fear neither the Pharisees nor those who are not Pharisees, but only the painted ones who resemble Pharisees." Whatever the case may have been, the Pharisees later persecuted the counselors of Jannaeus.

But this was under a new regime. Upon his deathbed (76 B.C.E.) Jannaeus transferred the royal dignity to his wife, Salome Alexandra, and is said to have advised her himself to alter the government's policy. She named her eldest son, Hyrcanus II, High Priest, and entrusted the government to the hands of the Pharisees. Those ordinances of the time of Hyrcanus which had fallen into desuetude were again put into force. Alexandra ruled in title only; the real power was in the hands of the Pharisees.

Having come into power, the Pharisees took vengeance upon the counselors of Jannaeus—who had recommended the crucifixion of the captives—by executing them. How did the Pharisees control the machinery of state? It appears that Alexandra introduced the scribes into the Sanhedrin, or council of state, where previously only the chief priests and members of the lay nobility had sat. Thus it was possible for the Pharisees, under the leadership of Simon ben Shetah, to employ the might of the state to overwhelm their opponents.

The anti-Pharisaic opposition consolidated itself under Alexandra and her second son, Aristobulus. As soon as the Queen died (67 B.C.E.) open war broke out between Aristobulus and his brother, Hyrcanus II, the legitimate successor. Aristobulus won. Hyrcanus renounced the throne, but soon sought to regain the crown with the help of the Arab Nabateans, to whom he promised to restore certain of the conquests of Jannaeus. His confidant and instigator in this struggle was Antipater the Idumean, father of the future King Herod. In the spring of 65 Aristobulus, occupying the Temple Mount, was besieged by Hyrcanus and his Arab allies and negotiations

170

were under way concerning the price of sacrificial victims that were necessary for the service in the Sanctuary.

But in the meantime the map of the world changed. Rome, which had long looked upon events in the East with indifference, was aroused by the conquests of King Mithridates of Pontus. In 66 Pompey defeated the Pontic king and also vanquished the Armenian Tigranes who then ruled Syria. When Pompey's legate Scaurus came to Damascus, he heard of the war between the brothers in Jerusalem. Scaurus hastened thither, and his expectations were realized. Both parties offered him money. He decided in favor of Aristobulus. The word of the Roman was sufficient cause for the Arabs to raise the siege.

But Scaurus was only the forerunner of one greater. In the spring of 63 Pompey himself came to Damascus. Again the Jewish parties appeared before him. Pompey postponed his decision. But Aristobulus feared that Pompey might in the end pronounce for Hyrcanus, who was supported by a numerous Jewish embassy. By his awkward conduct Aristobulus quickly lost the confidence of Pompey, who now ordered the occupation of Jerusalem. Aristobulus' supporters refused to admit the Romans,

171

but the party of Hyrcanus opened the gates of the city to them. The troops of Aristobulus, who had in the meanwhile been made captive by Pompey, again assembled on the Temple Mount. Pompey, supported by Hyrcanus, began the siege. In the fall of 63 the fortress was stormed and its defenders subdued. But even in the midst of the slaughter the priests continued the sacrificial service at the altar according to rule, paying no regard to the fury of the civil strife. They were struck down by the Romans at the very altar.

The proper history of the Maccabees thus comes to an end. Judea became a vassal princedom of the Romans. Hyrcanus II was at its head, no longer as king, however, but only as High Priest. As such, he lost the entire non-Jewish part of his realm, the acquisitions of Hyrcanus I and of Jannaeus. His princedom still included Judea, Samaria, Galilee, and Idumea, but was completely cut off from the sea by the coast cities liberated by Pompey. Most of Trans-Jordan too was lost to the Jews. Then in 40 B.C.E. Hyrcanus II was overthrown by the Parthians, led by his nephew Antigonus. Three years later Antigonus too was vanquished by the Romans, and Antipater's son Herod was entrusted with the rule of

Judea. Herod married Mariamne (Miriam), a grand-daughter of Hyrcanus II, and in 35 he made her brother Aristobulus High Priest; but in the following year he had him killed. In 30 he also caused the execution of the aged Hyrcanus, who since his fall from power had been living in Jerusalem as a private citizen. In the next year he also killed Mariamne, thinking she had been unfaithful to him. Next came the turn of Mariamne's mother, Alexandra. In 25 he caused the distant relatives of Hyrcanus to be tracked down and killed. Thus the last remnant of the house of the Hasmoneans was destroyed.

Historians since Flavius Josephus have been wont to ascribe the fall of the house to intestine strife. "Hyrcanus and Aristobulus were responsible for this disaster to Jerusalem. Therefore have we lost our liberty, and become subject to Rome." Others maintain that upon Alexandra "falls the responsibility for the rapid loss of the rule that had been achieved with such toil and danger," because she ruled according to the will of the enemies of the house, the Pharisees, repelling the true friends of the dynasty. This is obviously naive. When Pompey had once appeared in Syria, the subjugation of Jerusalem was inevitable. Rather, the quarrel between Hyrcanus and

Aristobulus saved Jerusalem from disaster. For now the Romans appeared in Judea as allies of at least one of the Jewish parties.

It was more important that Pharisaism had led to an estrangement of the people from the dynasty. Before Pompey at Damascus there appeared an embassy of Jews, who set forth to him that Rome had long been the protector of the Jews, who had thus enjoyed autonomy. Their head had been a High Priest, not a king. Their present Maccabean rulers, they declared, had enslaved the people and destroyed their ancestral constitution; they maintained their position only by terror and by the support of their soldiery. Later and in a precisely similar fashion, after the death of Herod, the Jews petitioned that none of the Herodians be named king, but that they be permitted to live without a king, according to the law of their fathers.

It is easy to see that the consistent Pharisees would sympathize with this position. To them it must have appeared that a foreign domination respecting Jewish autonomy and recognizing the Torah as the binding law of Judaism would offer less hindrance to their work of education. Precisely because it was foreign, and hence concerned only for the prompt payment of tribute and for civil order, they assumed that the internal life of the people would remain outside the range of its interest. According to Josephus, the people once pelted Alexander Jannaeus at the Feast of Tabernacles with *etrogim* (citrons), which are used in the ritual of that festival, because, as the son of a mother who had been a war captive, he was deemed unworthy of the priestly dignity. This objection was in keeping with the Pharisaic interpretation of the ordinances for the marriage of priests (Lev. 21:7). The Pharisees might justly expect foreign rulers scrupulously to follow the opinions of the scholars in all such matters whereas a Jewish king, as was the case with the Maccabees, would desire to shape even the internal and religious life of the people according to his own notions and not always according to the recommendations of the teachers of the law. In point of fact, it was the Roman rule which made possible and facilitated the development of Pharisaic Judaism to a high degree, until the great conflict between the two unequal powers set in. In this conflict the Jewish people lost its land, in order to win a historic continuity such as was vouchsafed to no other people of antiquity, not even to their conquerors, the Romans.

Who will venture to decide at this date whether, during the crisis after the death of Alexandra, one or the other of the Jewish political leaders was in the right? In the struggle between Aristobulus and Hyrcanus the partisans of the latter wished to have a wonder-worker named Honiah call down a solemn curse upon Aristobulus. But Honiah stepped forward between the contending parties and said: "O God, king of the universe, forasmuch as those standing about me are Thy people, but the besieged Thy priests, may it be Thy will neither to hearken to those against these, nor to fulfil what these pray against those." Can the historian of today judge otherwise than in the sense of this prayer concerning those who stood opposed to each other in hatred at the fall of the house of the Hasmoneans?

But the historian may deduce from the progress of history that precisely this estrangement of the people or its parts from the dynasty had great and, in the sequel, wholesome effects on Judaism. The subjugation of 63, by which the Jews again became subjects of an alien and pagan power, now no longer seemed a national and religious catastrophe that called forth despair for the future of the nation and the beneficence of God; rather, it seemed the just penalty for a dynasty of usurpers. In the apocryphal Psalms of Solomon, composed about this time, the Maccabees appear as wicked men who by violence occupied a throne not theirs but promised by God to the anointed of the house of David. The shoot of David, the promised Messiah, would one day crush the rulers and drive the heathen out; but not by earthly means, as the Maccabees wrongly thought they could do, but by the hand of God. "Happy is he whose help is the God of Jacob."

With the end of the Hasmoneans the messianic period of Jewish history begins.

———

The Maccabees saved Israel from the Greek danger. But this danger was twofold, and the Maccabees eradicated one kind of Hellenism only to facilitate the growth of another kind.

Hellenism was a supranational culture based upon reason and faith in reason. Hence its immediate effect upon all peoples whom it embraced was everywhere to disrupt tradition. If the Greek gymnasium in which naked youths indulged in sport was an abomination to the Maccabean Jew, in the same period the Elder Cato complains that the natural modesty of the Romans was being undermined by Greek athletic games; even during the Empire an old-fashioned Roman declares: "The relaxation of morals derives primarily from [Greek] cultivation of the body." In the Book of Maccabees the word "Hellenism" signifies "anti-Jewish." But in the Roman poet Plautus (died 184 B.C.E.) *pergraecari* ("to play the Greek") is virtually equivalent to "to be debauched." Cicero's grandfather used to say that the better a Roman spoke Greek, the more certain was he a scoundrel.

Contact with the "enlightened" and universal culture of Hellenism could only be salutary for one who, wrestling as Jacob did with the angel, did not allow himself to be overcome but extorted its blessing, not losing himself in Hellenism, but coming safely away with enhanced strength. Only two peoples of antiquity succeeded in doing so, the Romans and the Jews. The Romans succeeded because they became the rulers even of the Hellenic world. To be sure, they lost much in the process, a good part of their national religion, for instance, whose gods Greek gods supplanted. The Jews succeeded because their knowledge of the oneness of God and of His world rule—in a word, the singular character of their faith —set up an inner barrier against surrender and separated them from the rest of the world.

But separation alone could by its nature only preserve past gains; it could not enrich the spirit and the inner life. Many other Oriental peoples, as for example the Egyptians, shut themselves off from Hellenism; but this led only to their becoming backward; and their leading classes, seduced by Hellenism, were lost to the nation.

Jerusalem had been threatened with a similar fate. The leading men of Jewry went over to a foreign culture. The world of Hellenism offered hospitality, and they joined it at table. But by its prescriptions concerning the sacred and the profane the Torah interfered with this elegant love feast. The leading social class in Jerusalem therefore determined to abolish the separateness of the Jewish religion and its religious way of life, and if necessary to employ force in order to transform Judaism into a "philosophic" form of paganism. This was the party of the "reformers."

The Maccabees protested. They defended the God of their fathers against the deity fabricated by the reformers. By their uprising they preserved the uniqueness and permanence of Judaism, and they preserved monotheism for the world. The victory and reign of the Maccabees (after 152 B.C.E.) put an end to anti-Jewish Hellenism forever.

But the question of a final settlement with Hellenism had not been resolved. Hellenism continued to be a universal spiritual power, like Western civilization in the modern world—no people could isolate itself from it if it wished to live and assert itself. Above all, isolation would have involved a break with the already numerous communities of the Diaspora, which were scattered throughout the Greek world and hence were constrained to accept Hellenism.

180

With the Maccabees, then, the internal Jewish reconcilement with Hellenism begins. Ideas and concepts of the new age and the new culture were taken over without thereby surrendering native spiritual values. This was managed in two ways. First, the inner strengthening of the people achieved by the Maccabees made it possible to adopt unaltered ideas and institutions which had previously seemed to offer, or in fact did offer, a serious threat. John Hyrcanus was unwilling to admit a Seleucid garrison into Jerusalem because it was impossible for Jews and foreigners to live together. But he himself raised an army of foreign mercenaries. At the time of Epiphanes the gymnasium in Jerusalem was enormously dangerous to Judaism. In the time of Philo the Jews of Alexandria thronged the games without sacrificing any part of Judaism; and the theater, amphitheater, and hippodrome erected in Jerusalem by Herod were later visited even by orthodox Jews.

Secondly, Hellenistic notions were appropriated only after their poison had been drawn. The recipe was very simple: the new was fitted into the system of the Torah and was employed the better to serve the God of the fathers, not to elude Him the more adroitly. The sect of the Essenes, for example, which is mentioned as early as the turn of the second century B.C.E. and which was highly esteemed by the Jews, is a thoroughly Hellenistic growth upon Palestinian soil. In their organization, their moral practices, their usages, the Essenes imitated the Greek sect of the Pythagoreans. They even took it upon themselves to repudiate the sacrificial practices of the Temple. But all of this they subsumed under the Torah. They took the ancestral laws as their schoolmasters, zealously studied the Torah, honored Moses next to God, sent their offerings to the Temple, and in the Roman war accepted martyrdom rather than eat forbidden food.

Thus Judaism was able to enrich itself with new and foreign ideas and to be saved from the mummification that overtook the religion of the Egyptians, for example, which shut itself off from Hellenism completely. If today the West and Islam believe in resurrection, the idea is one which Maccabean Judaism took over from Hellenism and then passed on to Christianity and Islam.

The Maccabees preserved the Judaism of the Greek period from both dissolution and ossification. It is through their deeds that the God of Abraham, Isaac, and Jacob could and did remain our God. "My help cometh from the Lord, who made heaven and earth" (Ps. 121:2).

CHRONOLOGY

538: Return from the Babylonian Exile.

538-332: Palestine under Persian rule. Ezra and Nehemiah.

332: Alexander the Great conquers the Persian Empire, including Palestine.

3rd Century: Palestine under the rule of the Ptolemies of Egypt.

200: Antiochus III of Syria conquers Palestine.

187–176: Seleucus IV Philopator. The Wisdom of Jesus the Son of Sirach.

176: Antiochus IV Epiphanes.

175–172: Jason as High Priest. Beginning of the Hellenization of Jerusalem.

172–163: Menelaus as High Priest.

169: First Egyptian campaign of Epiphanes. The Temple plundered.

168: Rome conquers Macedonia. World dominion of Rome established.

168: Second Egyptian campaign of Epiphanes. Founding of Acra in Jerusalem.

167 (end): Temple desecrated; beginning of the persecutions.

166: Uprising of Mattathias.

165: Judah succeeds to the leadership. Book of Daniel. Campaign of Lysias.

164 (spring): End of the persecutions. Epiphanes' amnesty.

164 (end): Temple dedication. Inauguration of Hannukah.

163: Death of Epiphanes. Campaign of Eupator. Defeat of Judah.

162 (beginning):Treaty of peace. Alcimus as High Priest.

161: Judah's victory over Nicanor. Judah's alliance with the Romans.

160 (spring): Death of Judah.

159: Death of High Priest Alcimus.

152 (fall): Jonathan as High Priest.

146: Destruction of Carthage by the Romans.

142 (end): Death of Jonathan. Simon.

141 (spring): Conquest of Acra.

140: Simon as Ethnarch.

134: Death of Simon.

134–104: John Hyrcanus I.

134–133: Antiochus VII subdues Jerusalem but confirms its autonomy.

133: Beginning of the Gracchan revolution in Rome.

104–103: Aristobulus.

103–76: Alexander Jannaeus.

76–67: Salome Alexandra.

63: Pompey conquers Jerusalem.

THE HOUSE OF THE MACCABEES (HASMONEANS)

(167–29 B.C.E.)

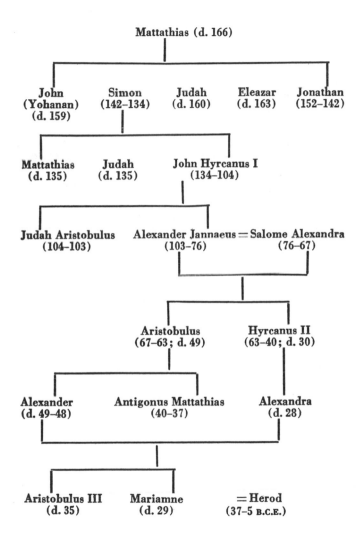

Mattathias (d. 166)

| John (Yohanan) (d. 159) | Simon (142–134) | Judah (d. 160) | Eleazar (d. 163) | Jonathan (152–142) |

Mattathias (d. 135) — Judah (d. 135) — John Hyrcanus I (134–104)

Judah Aristobulus (104–103) — Alexander Jannaeus (103–76) = Salome Alexandra (76–67)

Aristobulus (67–63; d. 49) — Hyrcanus II (63–40; d. 30)

Alexander (d. 49–48) — Antigonus Mattathias (40–37) — Alexandra (d. 28)

Aristobulus III (d. 35) — Mariamne (d. 29) — = Herod (37–5 B.C.E.)

THE SELEUCID KINGS
IN THE TIME OF THE MACCABEES

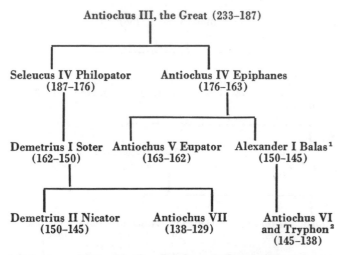

Antiochus III, the Great (233–187)

Seleucus IV Philopator (187–176)   Antiochus IV Epiphanes (176–163)

Demetrius I Soter (162–150)   Antiochus V Eupator (163–162)   Alexander I Balas[1] (150–145)

Demetrius II Nicator (150–145)   Antiochus VII (138–129)   Antiochus VI and Tryphon[2] (145–138)

[1] Balas passed himself off as Epiphanes' illegitimate son.

[2] Antiochus VI, while still a minor, was elevated to the throne by a man named Tryphon, who then waged war against Demetrius II in Antiochus' name.